JASPER JOHNS

EXHIBITION SCHEDULE

WHITNEY MUSEUM OF AMERICAN ART,
NEW YORK, NEW YORK
October 17, 1977–January 22, 1978

MUSEUM LUDWIG, COLOGNE, GERMANY
February 10–March 26, 1978

CENTRE NATIONAL D'ART
ET DE CULTURE GEORGES POMPIDOU,
MUSÉE NATIONAL D'ART MODERNE, PARIS, FRANCE
April 18–June 4, 1978

HAYWARD GALLERY, LONDON, ENGLAND
June 21–July 30, 1978

THE SEIBU MUSEUM OF ART, TOKYO, JAPAN
August 19–September 26, 1978

SAN FRANCISCO MUSEUM OF MODERN ART,
SAN FRANCISCO, CALIFORNIA
October 20–December 10, 1978

JASPER JOHNS

By Michael Crichton

HARRY N. ABRAMS, INC., PUBLISHERS, NEW YORK,
in association with the WHITNEY MUSEUM OF AMERICAN ART

The Jasper Johns exhibition was organized for
the Whitney Museum of American Art by David Whitney, assisted by David White.
Tom Armstrong, *Director* of the Whitney Museum, served as director of the exhibition.
They were assisted by Richard Marshall, *Assistant Curator, Exhibitions,* and
Patricia Westlake, *Secretary to the Director.*

The book was organized at Harry N. Abrams, Inc.,
by Patricia Egan, *Editor,* assisted by Heidi Colsman-Freyberger,
and by Patrick Cunningham, *Designer;*
at the Whitney Museum of American Art by Doris Palca, *Head, Publications and Sales,*
and Margaret Aspinwall, *Editor.*

Second Printing

Library of Congress Cataloging in Publication Data

Crichton, Michael, 1942-
  Jasper Johns.

  Bibliography: p.
  1. Johns, Jasper, 1930-   2. Artists—United
States—Biography. I. Johns, Jasper, 1930-
N6537.J6C74   709'.2'4   77-78150
ISBN 0-87427-024-3 **(PB)**
ISBN 0-8109-1161-2 **(HC)**

Printed and bound in Japan

Contents

Sponsor's Foreword

This exhibition was made possible by grants from
Philip Morris Incorporated and the National Endowment for the Arts.

Within the past quarter of a century, artists in America have initiated a succession of art movements that have attracted acclaim as well as controversy throughout the world. Among the outstanding things about this extraordinary period is that the combined vitality of artists, museums, and galleries has succeeded in generating an overwhelming response among large numbers of viewers. As the free pursuit of art in America was leading to the creation and exhibition of original and meaningful works, there was a simultaneous surge of free and vigorous appreciation among growing audiences. It is this interaction between the personal vision of the artist and the ultimate willingness of society to view art with an open mind that enables us today to honor an artist like Jasper Johns.

This exhibition of Johns' work represents a major milestone among the movements that first sprang forward in America in the 1950s. Along with others, Jasper Johns symbolizes the exciting "discoveries" in art made during those years, and still being made.

For some years, Philip Morris has been deeply concerned with the idea of a responsive and growing audience for art, and with providing the opportunities for such audiences to be exposed to and appreciate—or reject if they choose—the work of innovative artists. We are concerned also with bringing to the people in other countries the contributions of America's creative artists.

We at Philip Morris are grateful to the Whitney Museum of American Art for presenting this important exhibition, to David Whitney who served as curator, and to Michael Crichton for his incisive writing about the artist and his work. We are pleased and proud to be the sponsor of the exhibition together with the National Endowment for the Arts. It is a significant aspect of the collective effort involved that the show will travel to major museums in Cologne, Paris, Tokyo, and San Francisco through 1978.

Joseph F. Cullman 3rd
Chairman, Philip Morris Incorporated

Director's Foreword

In the finest sense of its purpose to show the best of American art, the Whitney Museum of American Art is proud to present an international traveling exhibition of the work of Jasper Johns and this book about the artist and his work. Since Jasper Johns and I first talked about the exhibition during lunch at Les Pléiades Restaurant in January 1975, he has been extremely helpful, and the entire project has benefited greatly from his enthusiastic cooperation.

David Whitney has been associated with Jasper Johns for many years and was his assistant from 1966 to 1968; Johns and I agreed that he would be the best person to organize the exhibition. He readily undertook to select the works, design the installation, accompany the exhibition as it traveled, as well as supervise the design of the book, assignments which have demanded his full attention for over two years.

In seeking someone to interpret Johns' work in the accompanying book, we wanted an author who would contribute an innovative understanding of the artist to the large and distinguished body of critical writing about him. Michael Crichton, who has known Johns and collected his work for some years and who needs no introduction as an author, accepted our invitation. We feel fortunate that we can provide this new view of the artist and discussion of his accomplishments.

It would have been impossible to present this exhibition and book without assistance from outside sources. The National Endowment for the Arts immediately honored our request for a grant, and we sought help from American business to match their endorsement. For more than twenty years, Philip Morris Incorporated has been a leader in supporting the arts, and we are pleased that they have joined us in this ambitious Whitney Museum project to exhibit the work of this American artist to an international audience. The generosity of Philip Morris, through the perceptive understanding of its management, has contributed toward making this presentation of the work of Jasper Johns as comprehensive as possible.

Leo Castelli presented Jasper Johns' first one-person exhibition in 1958, the year after opening his gallery. It seems appropriate that, during the twentieth anniversary year of the Castelli Gallery, we should celebrate an artist this dealer has worked with continuously since he first presented Johns' flags, targets, and numbers to the public. Castelli has been especially helpful with preparations for the exhibition and its international travel schedule. Tatyana Grosman and her staff at Universal Limited Art Editions have graciously assisted in the production of the cover of the book and the poster for the exhibition.

David Whitney has been assisted throughout the project by David White. He has also received kind cooperation from Mark Lancaster, Jasper Johns' assistant; at the Castelli Gallery, from Susan Brundage, Bradley Gillaugh, Louise Lawler, and Janelle Reiring; and at The Museum of Modern Art, from Cora Rosevear and Pearl Moeller. In putting the book together, Sally Welch Conner, Michael Crichton's assistant, helped with numerous details.

The staffs of the other museums presenting the exhibition have been particularly cooperative in assisting us to insure the finest care and best presentation of the works of art: Evelyn Weiss, Chief Curator, Wallraf-Richartz-Museum and Museum Ludwig, Cologne; Pontus Hulten, Director, Musée National d'Art Moderne, Paris; Ken-ichi Kinokuni, Acting Curator, and Yoshiaki Tono, Guest Curator for the Jasper Johns exhibition, The Seibu Museum of Art, Tokyo; Henry T. Hopkins, Director, San Francisco Museum of Modern Art. At the Whitney Museum nearly every staff member has worked on the exhibition, and I thank my associates for their untiring contribution to this outstanding event.

We are grateful to the lenders, who by parting with their works made this exhibition possible.

Tom Armstrong
Director
Whitney Museum of American Art

Introduction and Acknowledgments

"There is a deep question," writes psychologist Jerome Bruner, "whether the possible meanings that emerge from an effort to explain the experience of art may not mask the real meanings of a work of art."

That's one problem.

"Whatever you say about something," notes semanticist Alfred Korzybski, "it is not."

That's another problem.

The explanation of a joke is never funny.

That's a third problem.

This book attempts to thread a path through the logical minefield bordered by these concepts.

It is an outsider's attempt, but I am indebted to many people in the art world. One measure of Johns' excellence is the quality of the critical writing about him; I have drawn heavily on the work of three scholars in particular—Leo Steinberg, Max Kozloff, and Barbara Rose. Leo Castelli, Tatyana Grosman, and Ken Tyler talked with me at length about Johns. Robert Motherwell introduced me to the work of Anton Ehrenzweig. In preparing the manuscript I was assisted by the comments and suggestions of Mark Lancaster, David Whitney, Bob Gottlieb, Margo Leavin, Kurt Villadsen, Sally Welch Conner, and Arnold Mandell. Finally, Jasper Johns submitted cheerfully to many interviews over a period of eight months in 1976.

All these people have my profound thanks. Whatever errors and misconceptions remain in the text are mine.

M.C.
Los Angeles
January 1977

'We see, not change of aspect, but change of interpretation."
—Ludwig Wittgenstein

"I am just trying to find a way to make pictures."
—Jasper Johns

1.

Impressions of
THE ARTIST

Portrait of Jasper Johns, April 29, 1976, by Richard Avedon

I am waiting for an answer. Jasper Johns sits in an Eames chair in the room beneath his studio at Stony Point, New York. The walls are whitewashed and bare. He is a big, solid-looking man wearing faded jeans, a turtleneck sweater, and heavy boots. He stares out at the spring woods. His back is to the sunlight.

"I think you can be more than one person," he says finally. "I think *I* am more than one person. Unfortunately." And then he laughs.

Robert Hughes wrote: "Jasper Johns' face . . . resembles that of William S. Hart, the silent gunslinger of the silent Westerns. The narrow, crinkled eyes stare flatly, with an expression of ironic watchfulness, across the V of a gun-sight or the end of a paintbrush at—in either case—a target. It is the mask of cool, of a dandy who shuts up *and* puts up. What goes on behind that mask has provoked reams of critical speculation for more than a decade. . . ."[1]

HANDPRINT. 1964. Oil on paper, 53.2 x 43.8 cm (20⁵⁄₁₆ x 17¼"). Collection the artist

A recent interviewer wrote: "Johns is a highly intelligent, nervous and totally attentive personality. He speaks with great lucidity in King James version rhythms. . . . Questions are met by long silences, then answered with a precision that is partly legalistic, partly reminiscent of a dialogue with G. E. Moore. . . . He has a remoteness that, while very amiable, makes all questions sound vaguely coarse and irrelevant. . . . It is hard . . . to reconcile Johns' aura of sociability with the other impression of almost priestly apartness."[2]

A conversation with Jasper Johns has a quality difficult to describe, but so distinctive that people in the art world refer to "a Johnsian conversation." I will never forget my first.

Several years ago, Johns was making a series of lithographs at Gemini G.E.L. workshop in Los Angeles, based on his 1964 painting ACCORDING TO WHAT. Johns had begun by visiting the painting again, and he had had it photographed for reference, and he had taken some measurements. In this way he could use the same proportions for the prints. This seemed to me a slavish process, but Johns explained that by using these previous decisions, he was free to concentrate on other things as he made the prints. I watched carefully to see if I could determine what the "other things" were.

His method of working was not slow, but it was deliberate and punctuated by periods of staring. In fact, he seemed to welcome the hectic atmosphere of the print shop, where he was often interrupted by printers asking questions or needing a decision. Because his method had this stop-and-go quality, I thought it might be accessible to outside analysis, since I could view his work as a sequence of before-and-after steps.

Working on one print, he drew a spoon and a wire. He worked on the spoon handle for some time. However, after one of his judicious pauses, he changed it considerably. The handle was now different, but as far as I could tell, it was not different in any way that mattered. There was nothing to do but ask.

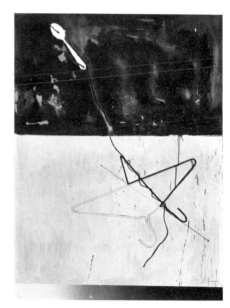

FRAGMENT—ACCORDING TO WHAT—COAT HANGER AND SPOON. 1971. Lithograph, 86.4 x 62.3 cm (34 x 25¼"). Published by Gemini G.E.L.

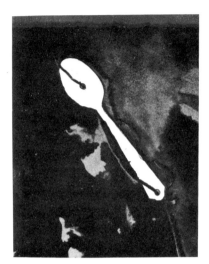

"Why did you make that change?"

"Because I did." His tone implied great reasonableness, as if that were the only possible answer.

I persisted: "But what did you *see?*"

"I saw that it should be changed."

Since I wasn't getting anywhere, I tried another approach. "Well, if you changed it, what was wrong with it before?"

"Nothing. I tend to think one thing is as good as another."

"Then why change it?"

By now he was getting exasperated with me. He sighed. There was a long pause. "Well," he said finally, "I may change it again."

"Why?"

"Well, I won't know until I do it."

The art critic Leo Steinberg has recorded another conversation: "I asked [Johns] about the type of numbers and letters he uses—coarse, stand-ardized, unartistic—the type you associate with packing cases and grocery signs.

Q: You nearly always use this same type. Any particular reason?

A: That's how the stencils come.

Q: But if you preferred another typeface, would you think it improper to cut your own stencils?

A: Of course not.

Q: Then you really do like these best?

A: Yes.

This answer is so self-evident that I wonder why I asked the question at all; ah yes—because Johns would not see the obvious distinction between free choice and external necessity. Let me try again:

Q: Do you use these letter types because you like them or because that's how the stencils come?

A: But that's what I like about them, that they come that way."[3]

A Johnsian conversation may be frustrating, but the artist is not being difficult. Quite the contrary: he struggles to find the plainest way of talking about a situation. His friend the composer John Cage recalls sitting on the porch at Johns' house in South Carolina, with "records filling the air with Rock-'n'-Roll. I said I couldn't understand what the singer was saying. Johns (laughing): That's because you don't listen."[4]

"He has the most literal mind of anyone I have ever met," said a critic at a dinner. Johns sat at the head of the table, not listening. This was several years ago when Johns wore a full beard, giving him an elegant, ducal appearance. It was difficult to avoid the feeling that night that Johns was holding court and the critic was banished to the far end of the table, excluded, and pretending not to care.

"I think that literalness shows in his work," the critic continued, more loudly. "He is a very puzzling man. He always takes you exactly at your word."

"How else should I take you?" Johns said, looking down the table.

"Oh, you know what I mean, Jasper."

"No," Johns said seriously, "I don't."

"There," the critic said, triumphant. "You see what I mean?"

"Whether or not you see what he means—and all that *that* means—is a central issue in Jasper's work," says a dealer. "Of course it reflects his personality. Jasper in person is very much like one of Jasper's paintings."

One night after dinner he offered to teach me to play backgammon. "I am a very good teacher," he said, "because I always lose."

"His work is a constant negation of impulses," said a critic who has known him a long time. "Wouldn't you say so, Jasper?"

"No," Johns said, and laughed.

"You should see how he works," said a friend. "I've seen it happen time and again. He'll make something that's just *beautiful,* it's so beautiful it makes your eyes water. But he puts it aside. Too pretty. Too easy. Too sensuous, too seductive. He isn't satisfied with that."

"Jasper is very elusive," said a critic, "but he wants to be found out."

"Have you found him out?"

"I don't think anybody has found him out," the critic said.

An old acquaintance of Johns', who had known him during his early days in New York in the fifties, called him up. The two had not seen each other in many years. Johns invited the man to dinner.

"We hardly said two words," the friend said afterward. "We had a nice dinner—he is a very good cook—and then we played backgammon all night until I went home. After all these years, we just played backgammon."

"It is difficult for him to talk," says a woman who has known him a long time. "But of course, that's why he is a painter. His *sensitivity* is what is so amazing. He is the most sensitive person I have ever met."

I am sitting with him in his living room in Stony Point. He is in the Eames chair; I am sitting on a couch. Between us is an opened book of his paintings; he has brought it out to make some point about the early targets.

The conversation has moved on to other things. As I frame my next question, I stare out at the green woods. My eye passes over the opened book, noticing the images, and I have a fleeting sense of irritation, of distraction. It is so quick I am hardly aware of it: it is something about the green woods and the red targets, the immediacy of nature and the small artificial reproductions. Almost subliminally I think, *I wish the book were closed.*

As I ask my next question, Johns reaches over and closes the book.

One must wonder about his sensory equipment, particularly his vision. During the seven years I have known him, he has complained about failing vision, and his occasional need to wear glasses.

"I think my vision is erratic. The doctor says my eyes are very good and I just want hyperacuity, which I used to have. I used to have incredible eyesight from close up to very far away. I saw incredible things when I was younger. I thought that what I saw was the way things looked, the way things were."

He says that he dislikes glasses because they "introduce a very unpleasant relative idea." He says that when he wears glasses, he always sees the frames.

He came to California for a week and the weather was bad. A friend drove him to the airport and apologized for the gray and gloomy weather. "That's all right," he said. "Gray is my favorite color."

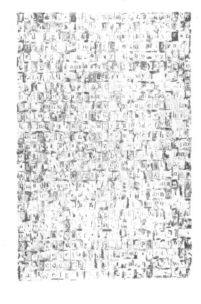

GRAY ALPHABETS. 1968. Lithograph, 152.4 x 106.7 cm (60 x 42"). Published by Gemini G.E.L.

His memory is remarkably specific. David Hockney was in Paris when Johns was there. "I asked him how he was liking Paris and he said that he wasn't. Hmm. Oh well, all right. I didn't see him again for months after that; he went back to the States, and I went to the South. Then I saw him in a restaurant. I asked him how he found Paris. He stared off into space the way he does, and then he slowly turned and looked at me, that slow way his head turns. 'You never give up, do you, David,' he said."

Moving through a garden, he is suddenly animated, alert. His ordinary diffidence and slowness are gone; his entire behavior changes. He bends over, he sniffs like a bloodhound, moving from plant to plant, touching, looking. He knows a great deal about growing things. He speaks quickly, gives advice about what to do, no pauses, no hesitation; he takes everything in at once. He seems to be at ease in the natural world, in a way he is not in an urban environment.

"You must remember that Jasper is really a Southern gentleman," said a dealer. "He has the most extraordinary, graceful manners. It's natural to him. You can see it around people he doesn't know, people he has no reason to pay attention to. He is very gentle, and very kind."

"He can be incredibly cruel. He can make you feel like *nothing.*"
"In what way?"
"It's impossible to describe, it's so subtle."

Once, when he was working at Gemini G.E.L., a senior printer suggested a change in one of Johns' prints. Johns replied mildly that he did not believe the change would improve the print. Astonishingly, the printer argued. Johns kept saying, "But I don't want to do that."

Later that day, the printer came in with a proof of a plate for Johns to look at. Johns was putting a wash on a stone; he was bent over the surface, his face just inches from it, his body taut, concentrating. The printer was ignored, and waited restlessly.

"Jasper, could you look at this?"

Absently, distracted, Johns looked up. In the same movement, he knocked the dish of black wash to the floor, where it splattered. For a moment nobody moved.

"Let me clean that up for you," the printer said.

"Thank you," Johns said pleasantly.

And with the printer crouched at his feet, cleaning up the spill, Johns looked at the proof. He said he liked it, and complimented the printer on his work.

"His method is to be oblique," says another woman. "He never comes right out and tells you. He *shows* you. He makes you see it for yourself. It's almost as if it's too painful for him to be direct."

He is direct about his work, an area of his life which he jealously guards. Once, at a dinner, a wealthy collector who owned several important Johns paintings announced over coffee that he had an idea for a print that Johns should do. He said that Johns should make a print, in color, of an American map. The collector argued his case cogently. He pointed out that Johns had done other prints in color based on paintings from that period; he alluded to the significance of such a print to the whole body of Johns' work; he mentioned the opportunities for the sort of image transformation which Johns' other color prints had explored; and he pointed out the peculiar arbitrariness that had led Johns to do map prints several times in black-and-white, but never in color.

A hush fell over the table. There was a good deal of tension. On the one hand, one doesn't tell an artist what to do, but on the other hand, the suggestion was not uninformed, and it did not come from a source the artist could casually alienate.

Johns listened patiently. "Well," he said finally, "that's all very well, but I'm not going to do it."

"Why not?" asked the collector, a little offended.

"Because I'm not," Johns said.

And he never has.

Driving in the car one day, he said, "I think artists are the elite of the servant class."

"He likes to play games," says an acquaintance. "He plays games all the time. He plays backgammon, he plays Monopoly, and he plays games in real life, too."

"What is remarkable about him is the way he never plays games," says

Two Maps II. 1966. Lithograph, 84.4 x 66 cm (33¼ x 26″). Published by ULAE

another painter. "I know he agonizes over decisions in painting, sometimes. But he makes up his mind and sticks to it. I admire that. He has a kind of acceptance that is extraordinary."

"Jasper plays with things," says Tatyana Grosman, at whose workshop, Universal Limited Art Editions, he has made more than a hundred prints. "He likes to see the choices. He plays, but he doesn't *try*. Jasper never tries. He does it. Nothing is half-spoken in his work. You only live once, there is no trying. You do it."

Of his working methods, he says, "I never developed good habits. I don't have discipline." He does not work every day, or at any particular hour. On the other hand, he is rigorous in a certain way. He only works on one painting at a time, he says, because he cannot know what to do next until the last painting is finished, and he has learned whatever he needs to learn from the experience.

His friend John Cage has written: "If it comes to his notice that someone else had one of his ideas before he did, he makes a mental or actual note not to proceed with his plan. (On the other hand, the casual remark of a friend can serve to change a painting essentially.)"[5] Cage should know. In 1959 Johns was working on the painting HIGHWAY, which contained the word of the title. Cage walked in and said, "You've put it right in the middle." Johns immediately painted out the letters, although they can still be discerned by the careful observer.

HIGHWAY. 1959. See Plate 66

I said, "I've never watched you paint."
   "Neither have I," he said, and laughed.

We are fortunate for this description of Johns at work, from John Cage: "He had found a printed map of the United States that represented only the boundaries between them. . . . Over this he had ruled a geometry which he copied enlarged on a canvas. This done, freehand he copied the printed map, carefully preserving its proportions. Then with a change of tempo he began painting quickly, all at once as it were, here and there with the same brush, changing brushes and colors, and working everywhere at the same time rather than starting at one point, finishing it and going on to another. It seemed that he was going over the whole canvas accomplishing nothing, and, having done that, going over it again, and again incompletely. And so on and on. Every now and then using stencils he put in the name of a state or the abbreviation for it, but having done this represented in no sense an achievement, for as he continued working he often had to do again what he had already done. . . . I asked how many processes he was involved in. He concentrated to reply and speaking sincerely said: It is all one process."[6]

MAP. 1961. See Plate 74

Johns visited his painting TENNYSON some years ago. He offered to buy it back from the owners, who did not want to sell. A woman was amazed by his

18

attitude. She said, "Well, if you want it so much, why don't you just make yourself one?" He could not explain why this was impossible. To do something again is to do it differently.

"How do you work on a painting?"
  "Well, I begin at the beginning, and go on from there."

Once I drove him from his house into New York City. We were going to some destination I did not know. I asked him how to get there. "Well, I'm not sure, I'll know when I see it, as we go."
  We drove for a while longer, crossing the George Washington Bridge. I asked again. "Well, I don't know. Turn right here, and we'll figure out the rest later."
  I became frustrated. I like to know where I am going, I like to plan ahead. He stays firmly in the present: we are going down this street now, and when we get to the end, we will decide which way to turn, and having decided that, we will wait until it is time to make another decision.
  We chatted about his family; he was relaxed, I was going crazy. But we finally arrived. We began at the beginning and went on from there.

"I can't play chess," he once said. "I don't have the right kind of head for it. I can't think of all those possibilities in advance."

Tatyana Grosman: "Once I visited Jasper in his studio. I talked about some work we had scheduled for the future. Jasper was vague and he kept looking out the window. Then I said, 'Oh, and I have these proofs for you to see.' Right away he is paying attention, very interested, no more looking out the window. So I said to him, 'Jasper, when I show you something, you are interested, but when I talk about the future you are bored.' He said yes. He said when he was young he had so many desires and wishes, that he trained himself to think only of the present, and not of his wishes for the future."

"I always wanted to sell a painting for a million dollars," he said once, after turning down an offer. There is that side to him: the man who at one time lived in a bank, and kept his paintings in the vault. He is an astute collector of his own work. The finest collection of Jasper Johns is owned by Jasper Johns. "I think that's to be expected," he says.

We prefer our artists to be naive children. The fact that Johns is so self-aware has exposed him to the charge that he manipulates the art world. This is a long-standing complaint about Johns. One museum curator reported a dream in which Jasper Johns spoke with quotation marks around every comment, "as if he was directing his remarks to art history, the way everything he says always is."

The art world is small, competitive, and full of double binds. If Johns becomes popular and paints as many canvases as he can sell, he is accused of

TENNYSON. 1958. See Plate 48

pandering to popular taste (an early criticism of his work).[7] On the other hand, if he declines to meet the demand for his work, he is manipulating the art world to raise his own prices. For Johns, with his fine sense of irony, there must be great irony here.

In the Museum of Modern Art, a woman said to him, "Jasper, you must be from the Southern Aristocracy."
   He said, "No, Jean, I'm just trash."
   She replied, "It's hard to understand how anyone who's trash could be as nice as you are."[8]

He hesitates to speak of the past, his childhood, his upbringing. It seems irrelevant to him, and in a sense we must accept this from an artist who is so explicitly impersonal in his work. "I have attempted to develop my thinking in such a way that the work I've done is not me—not to confuse my feelings with what I produced. I didn't want my work to be an exposure of my feelings."[9]

Tatyana Grosman: "I knew him so well through his work it never occurred to me to think about his background, where he came from. It was just his work, and what he represented in working. . . . Sometimes he would stop at the workshop on his way to someplace else, and sometimes he would stop on his way home. I lost track of when he was going, and when he was coming. It was just Jasper. There. Now."

He was born in Augusta, Georgia, on May 15, 1930. His parents separated after he was born. John Cage: "His earliest memories concern living with his grandparents in Allendale, South Carolina. Later, in the same town, he lived with an aunt and uncle who had twins, a brother and sister. Then he went back to live with his grandparents. After the third grade in school he went to Columbia, which seemed like a big city, to live with his mother and stepfather. A year later, school finished, he went to a community on a lake called The Corner to stay with his Aunt Gladys. . . . He stayed there for six years studying with his aunt who taught all the grades in one room, a school called Climax. The following year he finished high school living in Sumter with his mother and stepfather, two half sisters and his half brother. He went to college for a year and a half in Columbia where he lived alone. He made two visits during that period, one to his father, one to his mother. Leaving college he came to New York. . . ."[10]

As a young child living in his grandfather's house, he remembers being dressed in the kitchen, by the cook, in a new white linen suit. He didn't want to wear it, and threw off the suit, which landed in a skillet of hot grease on the stove. His grandfather came in and began throwing him in the air, catching him, and spanking him as he fell. He was terrified.

He lived with his grandfather, but his father lived in the same town and

Johns saw him intermittently. Once his father promised him his watch when he was grown up. Soon after, Johns decided that he was grown up; he went to his father's house and took the watch. His father came and took it back. "I guess I wasn't grown up, after all."

For as long as he can remember, he has wanted to be an artist. His grandmother had been an artist. He grew up with the idea that an artist was socially useful, as well as being "a good, exciting person."

A critic who has watched him paint said, "I think when he is working, Jasper is totally concentrated on those surfaces. He lives in those surfaces. The surfaces are his whole world, they are everything. He loses himself in them. They are everything."

A frequently cited passage from his notebooks reads:

> *Take an object*
> *Do something to it*
> *Do something else to it*
> *"   "   " " "*

WHITE TARGET. 1957. Encaustic on canvas, 75.9 x 76.2 cm (29⅞ x 30″). Whitney Museum of American Art, New York

As he once lived in a bank,[11] converted into a studio, he now lives in a rebuilt farmhouse—it had been moved in pieces to its present location—which he has changed in various ways. One way is particularly striking.

In both his upstairs studio and the room beneath it, he has used garage doors for walls. The garage doors are of the multi-hinged variety that slide on overhead tracks. When the doors are closed, they form the walls of his house. When he opens them, they slide up toward the ceiling, and thus open the house to the breezes of the woods.

He has left the doors with all their galvanized handles, the manufacturer's plates, intact. He has also left the curving overhead tracks exposed. Thus the doors are both walls and doors, at the same time.

Yet the doors serve a transformed function, and they are literally changed; they have glass panels instead of wood, and this means they were specially constructed. (He thinks; he isn't sure.)

When asked how he came to have garage doors for walls, he is characteristically diffident. A friend suggested it, and an architect carried out the design.

Photograph of Interior of Jasper Johns' House, Stony Point, N.Y.

More transformations: Johns is almost inherently elegant, but at meals he employs the heavy white ceramic dishware that is usually found in the cheapest cafeterias; wine is served in the little shot-glasses of tawdry French *boîtes*. By using these commonplace articles in another setting, he makes you see them freshly for the first time, makes you perceive their beauty.

But it is a ready-made beauty, a commonplace beauty, a beauty which Johns has nothing to do with—except that he shows it to you.

"There are evidently more persons in him than one,"[12] wrote his friend John Cage. And the contrasts are striking—the reclusive logician who can be charming and outgoing; the self-conscious artist who proceeds by intuition; the intellectual who will not explain himself in intellectual terms; the tendency to obliqueness and the tendency to literalness; the man who has been called both generous and perverse; the creator of enigmatic work based upon mundane imagery; the ascetic who is a marvelous cook; the man who says that most of his life is haphazard and accidental, but allows no accidents in his pictures; the artist who undoubtedly strives to convey doubt.

These contrasts are not only striking. In many ways, they are what his work is about.

NOTES

1. Robert Hughes, "Jasper Johns' Elusive Bull's-Eye," *Horizon,* 14, Summer 1972, p. 21.
2. Vivian Raynor, "Conversation with Jasper Johns," *Art News,* 72, March 1973, pp. 20–22.
3. Leo Steinberg, "Jasper Johns: The First Seven Years of His Art" (1962), *Other Criteria: Confrontations with Twentieth-Century Art,* Oxford University Press, New York, 1972, p.32.
4. John Cage, "Jasper Johns: Stories and Ideas," in *Jasper Johns,* exhibition catalogue, The Jewish Museum, New York, 1964, p. 21.
5. *Idem.*

6. *Ibid.,* p. 22.
7. Hilton Kramer: "Johns, like Rauschenberg, aims to please and confirm the decadent periphery of bourgeois taste." ("Month in Review," *Arts,* 33, Feb. 1959, p. 49.)
8. Reported in Cage, *op. cit.,* p. 21.
9. Raynor, *op. cit.,* p. 22.
10. Cage, *op. cit.,* p. 23.
11. The actual location was a former New York Provident Loan Society building.
12. Cage, *op. cit.,* p. 22.

2.

A Brief History of
THE WORK

We can think of any artist as concerned with one question, one issue, one central theme, which he circles around, elaborates upon, and explores all his working life. This is easiest to see in artists who work in narrative forms. Hemingway never strays far from the masculine anxieties embodied in his first character, Jake Barnes; Hitchcock reiterates his domestic fears; Arthur Penn is haunted by paternal images; Stanley Kubrick is obsessed with obsession; Fitzgerald plays out desires destined to be unfulfilled; Joseph Heller cares for trapped, repetitive lives—the list could be extended indefinitely, into other areas and backward in time. The point remains the same. Art is a compulsive activity in which the artist attempts to rationalize, and come to grips with, some inner source of conflict.[1] The fact that most artists are unaware of their core concern; the fact that they usually attempt to present their work freshly, with a semblance of newness; the fact that they may work for ordinary goals such as money, fame, attention, should not obscure the basic nature of their enterprise, and its deeply monomaniacal quality.

Visual artists are as singleminded as any other; in the twentieth century, with the benefit of—and competition from—mechanical reproduction techniques, the compulsive, repetitive nature of the visual artist has become particularly clear.[2]

What, then, is the central concern of Jasper Johns? One answer is perception. Of course, all painters are concerned with perception, just as all racing drivers are concerned with engine mechanics. But with Johns, the issues of perception—of what you see, and why, and how you decide what you are looking at—are not merely questions to be decided in order to produce some final effect. They are, instead, the focus of the work itself. There is no final effect beyond these issues. There are only the issues, made concrete in one form or another.

This is why Johns has been called "an artist's artist"; and it is one reason why he has been such an influential force among other twentieth-century artists. This is also why he has been the subject of some of the most intense and difficult critical writing ever produced. For a painting by Johns often, by its very presence, suggests the question, what is painting? And his use of color often makes one ask what color really is. Or an object may be attached to the canvas in such a way as to throw doubt onto the meaning of the object—even when it is commonplace, a cup or a broom or a fork.

Now one can say that good art is always, at least in part, a commentary on art. But with Johns, this feature is carried to a kind of ruthless extreme, to the point where his most recent paintings suggest a psychological test of perception, and a test on the most fundamental level.

Johns is a serious and difficult artist who makes no apologies for the difficulties he creates. But he is also a humorous artist, and something about his method makes it intriguing to consider the most aggravating and abstract issues of art. (This is another reason why so much has been written about him.) From his first public showing, he has also been a popular artist, a playful technician who proposed a game the viewer eagerly participated in. In a sense, all art is instruction—Johns has said he regards his paintings as information—and he emerges as a teacher, with an implied didactic function that all good art possesses. The question, now, is how this original artist found himself, his working methods, and his audience.

The mass communication techniques of the twentieth century have transformed art, as they have transformed everything else. The discoveries that an artist makes are instantaneously transmitted around the world. We do not have to wait to see the evolution of a man's thought; we are witness to every step of the process, and every intermediate discovery has its impact on other artists, and on society as a whole. This is one reason why artists no longer need to be dead in order to be influential; and it is one reason why the pace of artistic evolution has accelerated, along with the pace of other advances, in the twentieth century. Indeed, for a modern artist there is a new problem that would have astounded his counterparts of past centuries, who were constantly hungry for attention. For the modern artist, there is sometimes a need to hide, to avoid the scrutiny of the disseminating mass media, until a new phase of work and thinking has been fully evolved.

Or perhaps it is not really so new. Leonardo da Vinci wrote that, in order to paint, one required isolation.[3] What he meant was freedom from the artist's natural tendency to respond to outside influences, suggestions, praise, criticism. Artists are, after all, creatures who respond to their environment in peculiarly brisk and subtle ways. And to be original—to break from the past, from tradition—almost demands isolation.

UNTITLED. c. 1953. Oil and collage on silk, 22.5 x 22.5 cm (8⅞ x 8⅞″). Collection Edwin Janss, Thousand Oaks, California

It is a peculiarity of Jasper Johns' life in the middle of the twentieth century that he passed his early, formative years in virtual isolation—only a few people cared about his work, and he saw little work by other artists. For the most part he painted alone. But this fortuitous start did not protect him from the subsequent series of life crises that characterize any significant artist. How, then, did he begin?

One day in 1954, Jasper Johns, then twenty-four, methodically destroyed all the work in his possession. This was the first of several acts of self-destruction by an artist who would eventually be known for his skill and daring at rebuilding his past.

Nevertheless he wiped out most of our earliest clues to his concerns. Just four pieces that survived—they were in the hands of others—provide insight into his formative interests.

UNTITLED (c. 1953) is a small square oil and collage on silk, an array of green rectangular strips in a grid-like pattern.[4] CONSTRUCTION WITH TOY PIANO (1954) is a collage incorporating a toy piano, its keys at the top of the composition. The keys are numbered; when pressed, they make sounds.[5] A third, UNTITLED (c. 1954), is a collage of printed matter in a box, with a cast woman's face at the bottom.[6] STAR (1954) is a Jewish star made of a variety of materials—canvas, wood, glass, encaustic.[7]

Reviewing these early efforts, the critic Max Kozloff observed: "What can be deduced about the creator of these virtual cabinet pieces is a predilection

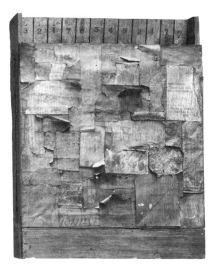

CONSTRUCTION WITH TOY PIANO. 1954. Graphite and collage with objects, 27.9 x 22.9 cm (11 x 9″). Private collection

for compartmental divisions, stained surfaces, and nostalgic references. . . . He creates memento boxes. . . ." And while Kozloff notes that the appearance of the numbers, the incorporation of the cast face, and the ambivalent attitude toward the surface "presage the artist to come," he concludes that "these are fragmented, rather precious objects," and compares them unfavorably to the work of Joseph Cornell.[8]

At the time Johns destroyed his work, he had been living in New York for a year, since his Army discharge. He had come to the city to continue college, but after the first day—a lecture on *Beowulf,* a French lesson, and a drawing class—he quit. He worked in a bookstore and painted sporadically. In general, his life seems to have been uncertain, tentative, unfocused. There was a sense of waiting.

Then came the day when he tore everything up. It coincided with what he has called a spiritual change: "Before, whenever anybody asked me what I did, I said I was going to become an artist. Finally I decided that I could be going to become an artist forever, all my life. I decided to stop *becoming,* and *to be* an artist."

One recalls the boy who decided he was grown up enough to claim his father's promised watch. But in this case the decision held; there was a profound change, and it implied not only a commitment to work, but also a method. "I decided to do only what I meant to do, and not what other people did. When I could observe what others did, I tried to remove that from my work. My work became a constant negation of impulses."

His attitude recalls the views of another Southerner, Edgar Allan Poe: "The fact is, that originality (unless in minds of very unusual force) is by no means a matter, as some suppose, of impulse or intuition. In general, to be found, it must be elaborately sought, and although a positive merit of the highest class, demands in its attainment less of invention than negation."[9] But Johns has never shown much interest in novelty per se, and his "negation of impulses" was not so much a search for originality as it was a young man's quest for self-identity in working. It is impossible to miss both the arrogance and the anxiety of youth when he says: "I had a wish to determine what I was. I had the feeling that I could do anything. . . . But if I could do anything I wanted to do, then what I wanted to do was find out what I did that other people didn't, what I was that other people weren't. . . . It was not a matter of joining a group effort, but of isolating myself from any group. I wanted to know what was helpless in my behavior—how I would behave out of necessity."

The quality of negation—so much discussed in Johns' later work—is thus clearly expressed from the start. So is the sense of isolation. At this time, he had little money and few friends; he did not know many artists and had seen very little art of any sort. In the most literal sense, he was a naive and provincial artist from South Carolina, working alone in New York City, following his inner impulses with the only tools he had—a ruthless logical sense, and technical virtuosity.

He was willing to try anything ("I did everything I could think to do") but two technical interests were later to prove particularly important. One was

UNTITLED. c. 1954. Construction, oil, and collage with plaster cast, 66.6 x 22.2 cm (26¼ x 8¾"). Collection Rachel Rosenthal Moody

STAR. 1954. Encaustic on canvas with glass and wood, 57.5 x 50.2 cm (22⅝ x 19¾"). Private collection, Los Angeles

the use of encaustic—a difficult, seldom-employed technique in which, essentially, pigment or collage elements mixed with hot wax are applied to a surface. Johns has always been attracted to the most demanding technical challenges, and certainly the difficulty of encaustic must have been appealing to him. But he recalls that he began to use wax to solve a problem:

"It was very simple. I wanted to show what had gone before in a picture, and what was done after. But if you put on a heavy brushstroke in paint, and then add another stroke, the second stroke smears the first unless the paint is dry. And paint takes too long to dry. I didn't know what to do. Then someone suggested wax. It worked very well; as soon as the wax was cool I could put on another stroke and it would not alter the first."

A second interest was plaster casting. He apparently made casts of heads and body parts—of himself, of friends—in part because of a sort of exuberant fascination with the process itself.

If Johns' early work was reminiscent of Joseph Cornell, he soon embarked upon a course of investigation uniquely his own. In 1954, he had a dream in which he saw himself painting a large American flag; soon after, he did his first one.

FLAG. 1955. See Plate 1

In that impersonal image he found his self-identity. ("It was something I could do that would be mine.") The first flag was made in encaustic, a technique that would be later identified as his, too. But immediately a sense of Johnsian paradox inserts itself—how can a young artist believe that he has found himself in painting an image that nobody owns, that is not uniquely identified with anyone (except perhaps Betsy Ross), and that possesses a meaning, or an emotional content, which is obscure to say the least? Nevertheless this was Johns' opinion, and it is a tribute to his artistic force that subsequent years proved him correct—the American flag became "his" image in a way that nobody challenged.

Painting the first flag triggered many related ideas. "Using the design of the American flag took care of a great deal for me because I didn't have to design it. So I went on to similar things like the targets—things the mind already knows. That gave me room to work on other levels."[10]

What other levels? The question is critical to Jasper Johns' method of operation. If he does not have to create an image, but uses ready-made designs, images, and lettering, what does his work consist of?

We have a clue in a further elaboration: the flags and targets are similar because "they're both things which are seen and not looked at, not examined, and they both have clearly defined areas which could be measured and transferred to canvas."[11]

There are two points: first, the notion of something which is seen and not seen, because of familiarity. And second, the idea of something which can be accurately measured and put onto canvas—something with fixed proportions. How do these ideas go together? On a simple level, because an accurately reproduced flag is familiar, and therefore "not looked at." But more is involved here—no artist wants his work to be "not looked at." Quite the reverse is true. If it is a politician's first duty to be elected, it is an artist's first duty to be looked at. Therefore we are presented with a paradox—in what way can a familiar, reproducible image become something that is to be looked at freshly?

The simplest answer is technique, the way the image is made. An actual flag is flat cloth; the flag image is a flat abstraction. By painting the image in encaustic, with its heavily worked, encrusted surface, the flag image becomes something familiar and unfamiliar at the same time, and therefore worthy of our notice.

This treatment of a mundane image provokes two further, more intellectual puzzles. One concerns the idea of painting a flag. In the 1950s that seemed to many observers an absurdity: the American flag is many things, but it is certainly not art. Yet Johns presents a carefully worked, elegantly done painting. Such a painting is surely art—or is it? That becomes a problem for the viewer. Johns has already done the painting, he has already presented the problem. The viewer is left to resolve it, as best he can.

The second paradox lies in the idea of "things seen and not looked at." Here is a conversation at 221B Baker Street:

"... And yet I believe that my eyes are as good as yours."

"Quite so," he answered, lighting a cigarette, and throwing himself down into an arm-chair. "You see, but you do not observe. The distinction is clear. For example, you have frequently seen the steps which lead up from the hall to this room."

"Frequently."

"How often?"

"Well, some hundreds of times."

"Then how many are there?"

"How many! I don't know."

"Quite so! You have not observed. And yet you have seen. That is just my point. Now, I know that there are seventeen steps, because I have both seen and observed."[12]

In the same way, we can ask how many red stripes there are in an American flag.

Johns' painted targets explored ideas suggested by the early flags, but more abstractly. An American flag is always the same, while a target can be any number of things—all that unites targets is a common format of concentric circles. A flag is bound to one nation; a target is universal. The colors of the flag are fixed; in the target, they need only be contrasting.[13]

The target also focuses attention on the theme of viewing. After all, the contrasting circles of the target are there for the purpose of aiding distant vision; the target is something to see clearly, to aim at. In short, the target is a true visual display—it has no other purpose, no other reason for existence. (Blind archers shoot at a "target" of sound.)

But in his first target painting, Johns went beyond any simple treatment of targets as a symbol. TARGET WITH PLASTER CASTS (1955) joins the collage target with plaster casts of body parts, set behind hinged doors above the bull's-eye. He is aware of echoing a composition from the earlier CONSTRUC-

TARGET WITH PLASTER CASTS. 1955. See Plate 7

29

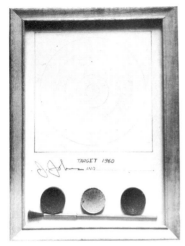

TARGET. 1960. Pencil on board with brush and watercolor disks, 17.1 x 11.8 cm (6¾ x 4⅝"). Private collection

TARGET WITH FOUR FACES. 1955. Encaustic and collage on canvas with objects, 75.5 x 66 cm (29¾ x 26"). The Museum of Modern Art, New York. Gift of Mr. and Mrs. Robert C. Scull

TANGO (detail). 1955. See Plate 13

TION WITH TOY PIANO, in which the rectangular keys appear at the top of the image; it is interesting that he originally intended the hinged doors to be keys, attached to wires that ran behind the canvas. When you pressed one of the trap-door "keys" a sound would issue from the canvas target. But Johns abandoned this idea when he couldn't think of a suitable hidden mechanism for making sound. Then he substituted the casts of body parts, painted in different colors. The colored rectangles reminded him, he says, of water-color sets with their dishes of paint—an association he made explicit in TARGET (1960), which includes paints and a brush beneath the concentric circles.

In the smaller TARGET WITH FOUR FACES (1955), cut-off plaster casts stand above the target surface. The faces are all the same woman, cast serially. In each successive casting, the woman was more relaxed and the mouth more open; he was forced to rearrange the casts so that there was no sense of a progression, of "a mouth about to speak," which he did not want.

What did he want? A hint comes from TANGO, painted the same year. A significant feature of TANGO is the incorporation of a music box into the painting, with an exposed key to be wound. The music box originally played *Silent Night,* but he altered it so it just made plinking sounds.[14] With both TANGO and the targets, "I wanted to suggest a physical relationship to the pictures that was active. In the targets, one could stand back or one might go very close and lift the lids and shut them. In TANGO, to wind the key and hear the sound, you had to stand relatively close to the painting, too close to see the outside shape of the picture."

In other words, Johns was already aware of trying to influence the observer—in this case, to influence the observer's physical position in rela-tion to the painted surface. And he did it by providing a temptation, a source of curiosity, a reason to move closer and then to step back. The painting provokes an interaction with the observer: it takes two to tango.

There is another interesting feature of TANGO—the fact that the painted surface stops "indiscreetly"[15] short of the bottom of the canvas, suggesting a distinction between what is painted and what underlies the painted surface. Johns has used this device in many paintings since—including the recent THE BARBER'S TREE (1975)—but he discovered it with TANGO: "In painting a large canvas, it was too hard to reach down to the bottom, to bend over. So I just didn't do it. Then when I noticed what I had done, I decided I liked it, and left it."

Is this an accident? Johns would say that it is not, since—once he noticed what had happened—he had the option of changing it. Therefore to leave it is no accident. It becomes intentional, a choice. But the way this choice presents itself is accidental, in the sense that Johns' original idea for the painting TANGO did not include the exposed canvas at the bottom. That was a discovery in the course of working which he allowed to remain. The fact that he was aware of this discovery, and utilized it, tells us a great deal about his method of creation; he is willing to permit what has happened in working to remain as a permanent feature of the work. He does not always do this, of course—in that sense he is wrongly perceived as an "action painter." In fact, many paintings demonstrate the most laborious efforts to cover previous mistaken decisions.[16]

In 1955 he also painted his first numbers. Given an artist interested in flat, mundane imagery, the choice of numbers as a subject seems obvious. But it is actually a further step into abstraction. After all, an American flag has a physical reality—the reality of the rippling flag atop the pole. Johns never paints a rippling flag; he sticks to the design itself, and makes a "thing" that hangs on the wall, calling attention to itself. But it does have a reference to a physical object in the environment. Similarly, targets do exist, in various forms for various purposes.

But numbers are different. Numbers exist only in the imagination. We write them every day, we use them all the time, but they remain stubbornly abstract in a peculiar way. Johns paints his numbers as if they had some inherent concrete reality—and indeed the very act of painting produces a kind of concrete reality. What is that painting? It is a painting of the number 7, the shape of the numeral, standing without a context. Cézanne painted seven apples; Johns just paints 7.[17]

Such lack of context for the "subject," the painted figure, makes us acutely aware of the painting itself as a physical object. This has always been important to Johns. Early in his career, he said that people should be able to look at a painting "the same way you look at a radiator,"[18] in other words, an ordinary object. No special vision was required. Just look at the thing and see what it was.

This is, of course, a very deceptive attitude. For the moment we will only point out that the artist's stance almost obliges him to work with recognizable, mundane imagery. But he quickly began to alter his everyday images in unexpected ways.

After the first red, white, and blue American flag, Johns painted WHITE FLAG, on a huge scale, using the same technique, but this time without the color. WHITE FLAG, which Max Kozloff has called "a fossil,"[19] is in fact an enormously impressive painting—perhaps the most blatantly sensuous canvas Johns has ever produced.

Soon after, he did FLAG ABOVE WHITE, in which he extended his concerns in a significant way. "Originally the shape of the canvas was determined by the subject matter. Then I tried to extend the surface beyond the subject matter—or what most people would call the subject matter."

In summary, the work of 1955 represents an extraordinary effort. In a single year, we see a man of twenty-five take one idea—an American flag on a canvas—and push it, stretch it, extend it, with great invention and inexorable logic. Even today there is a taut, controlled excitement about these pictures that cannot be missed.

It must have been an exciting year in his life, as well. By 1955, Johns was living in a loft on Pearl Street in New York, and Robert Rauschenberg moved into the same building. Rauschenberg was five years older than Johns and he already had a reputation as a provocative and irritating, although personally engaging, young man; he had appeared in *Life*

Paul Cézanne. *Apples*. 1873–77. Collection Lady Keynes, London

FIGURE 7. 1955. See Plate 5

FLAG ABOVE WHITE. 1955. Encaustic on canvas, 55.9 x 48.3 cm (22 x 19″). Private collection

Robert Rauschenberg and Jasper Johns

magazine, and had had several shows. In one he had exhibited pictures made of dirt, which caused no end of consternation. And although it was not yet widely known, he had done something even more startling: he had erased a de Kooning drawing and called the result his own work.

Rauschenberg and Johns were close friends, although they were different in nearly every imaginable way. Rauschenberg was voluble and outgoing where Johns was reserved; Rauschenberg was explosively energetic where Johns was patient and deliberate; Rauschenberg was hectic where Johns was elegant and precise; Rauschenberg was exasperating and shocking where Johns never desired to shock. Nevertheless the two men shared certain characteristics: both Southern, both oddly naive, both impoverished and struggling.

Their closeness led them, on occasion, to paint each other's pictures. Johns said: "When you are young, you think you can do anything. I didn't see why I couldn't do a Rauschenberg if I wanted to. So I tried once or twice. But it didn't work; someone saw my Rauschenbergs and noticed there was something funny about them."

It is a curious comment on youthful bravado, but it is also true that Johns and Rauschenberg shared certain attitudes toward art which led them, when they both finally became established, to be discussed together as "neo-Dadaists." The similarity of their attitudes led more than one critic to see their work as similar; Johns was occasionally criticized for a Rauschenberg canvas.[20]

What, exactly, did they share? A belief that art sprang from life experiences, but that the painter was not obliged to be "self-expressive" in the manner then popular; a belief that the commonplace should be incorporated into art; a belief that in looking at art, you should see whatever you ordinarily saw; and a belief that the hard distinction between representation and abstraction masked an ambiguous area of great interest to both of them.

Beginning in the 1950s, Johns and Rauschenberg worked for a period of several years in close association, seeing each others' work daily, and they supported each other in a time of isolation. Rauschenberg said later that they gave each other "the permission to do what we wanted."[21]

Through Rauschenberg, Johns met another important figure in his life, the composer John Cage. Cage was considerably older than either man; Rauschenberg had known him from his time at Black Mountain College in North Carolina. Johns, who considers Cage "my best friend," has said: "Knowing John had a great effect on my work. He is a presence that is still very important in a group of friends that I have. John is intellectually generous and also he has a kind of tendency to teach which is useful to other people. He is capable of grasping ideas in different disciplines and making relationships among them. He is probably the first person I met who took such pleasure in ideas."

In Johns' work it is almost impossible to trace out Cage's influence in any simple way; perhaps the strongest influence lies in attitudes toward work and life. Johns himself has said that any influence from Cage came more from living, than from talk about art. For example:

John Cage.
Photograph by James Klosty

"Whenever I was stopped from what I wanted to do, I would get frustrated. John never does. One day we were driving on the New Jersey turnpike. It was raining; the car went through a deep pool of water and stalled. I was furious. John didn't mind at all. We got the car over to the side of the road. Then John took out a scrabble game and we had a sort of party until the engine dried and we could go on. His attitude was really much better: there was no point getting upset since there was nothing we could do. But you don't think to act that way, unless you see someone else doing it."

Association with Cage brought Johns another friend, the choreographer and dancer Merce Cunningham. For many years Johns has worked in some capacity with the Merce Cunningham Dance Company; he has been involved in fund-raising efforts, has designed costumes, and on one occasion designed a set based on Duchamp's *Large Glass*.[22] Johns is a retiring man whose own dramatic sense is finely muted; when he talks of the Cunningham company one senses an undercurrent of fascination and pleasure at the idea of an art that leads to public performance.

But he has never been drawn to perform himself. Once, in Paris, several artists performed during a concert,[23] but Johns did not even appear onstage; he sent a floral wreath in the shape of a target as a stand-in for his own presence. It is a gesture rich with suggestion—wreaths are appropriate, after all, for holidays and funerals, triumphs and tragedies;[24] and Johns has always been preoccupied with the idea of the stand-in, with the surrogate, with one thing representing another; a recent painting, THE DUTCH WIVES (1975), explicitly takes up this notion.

Merce Cunningham.
Photograph by James Klosty

In restrospect, the primary influence of the middle 1950s was Rauschenberg, the gregarious, frustrating, instantaneously brilliant Rauschenberg.[25] Johns said: "Bob was the first person I knew who was a devoted painter, whose whole life was geared to painting. I had never met anyone like that."

He had never met a devoted painter? In such comments, we glimpse Johns' youthful isolation: an isolation that continued for several years to come. He recalls working for three more years—"It seemed like a *very* long time"—with an audience of only a handful of people who saw and commented upon his work.

During this time he patiently elaborated upon his previously determined themes—the mundane image, the flat abstraction, "the things the mind already knows," the painting-as-object. There was no sign, yet, that anything was wrong, no evidence for the dissatisfaction that would eventually cause him to change drastically his own working methods and concerns.

The years 1956–57 mark the first use of objects attached to the painted surface—with the works CANVAS, BOOK, and DRAWER. The fact that the attached objects were painted over, as if they were part of the original surface, draws attention to, and throws doubt upon, the meaning of surface in a disturbing way. The effect is heightened by painting the sides of the canvas as well, something he did often during this period.[26] His treatment again emphasizes the idea of the painting as a physical object hanging on the

FLORAL DESIGN. 1961. Pencil, watercolor, and collage on paper, 56.5 x 47.9 cm (22¼ x 18⅞"). Collection the artist

33

FLAG ON ORANGE FIELD. 1957. See Plate 22

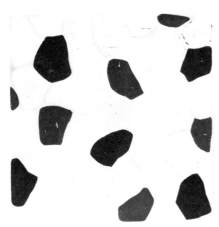

HARLEM LIGHT (detail). 1967. See Plate 129

Claude Monet. *Poppy Field near Giverny.*
1885. Museum of Fine Arts, Boston

wall. "One of the extreme problems of paintings as objects is the other side—the back. It can't be solved; it's in the nature of the work." His concern with surfaces and "the other side" continued for several years more, in a series of paintings that include GRAY RECTANGLES (1957), SHADE (1959), DISAPPEARANCE (1960), and DISAPPEARANCE II (1961).

Also in 1956, Johns did the first of his alphabets, further extending his repertoire of ordinary flat imagery. The arrangement of GRAY ALPHABETS is straightforward, the effect reminiscent of a typographer or an ophthalmologist—someone who cares about the letters for more than their usual, literal, meaning.

In 1957, he also began to work with an image and a surrounding color field, with FLAG ON ORANGE FIELD. Of this work, the critic Barbara Rose has said: "Between the early and later works lie a number of transitional paintings. . . . Perhaps the most important of these . . . is the *Flag on Orange Field.* A punning title, presumably a pun on 'flag' as a synonym for iris, links the painting semantically with the later pun on 'flags' in the flagstones of red, white, and black in [HARLEM LIGHT (1967)[27]] paintings of 1968. If we accept the flower image established through a pun, Monet's *Field of Red Poppies* comes to mind as a possible source for the sunny Impressionist landscape Johns has created. In *Flag on Orange Field,* several new elements are introduced. Although the flag is still an *a priori* image, a context, of which the original flags were deprived, is introduced in the form of the Impressionist field which acts as a frame for the flag."

In an interview, some years ago, Johns said: "*Flag on Orange* was involved with how to have more than one element in the painting and how to be able to extend the space beyond the limits of . . . the predetermined image. . . . It got rather monotonous, making flags on a piece of canvas, and I wanted to add something—go beyond the limits of the flag, and to have different canvas space. I did it early with the little flags with the white below, making the flag hit three edges of the canvas and then just adding something else. And then in the *Orange,* I carried it all the way around."[28]

It got rather monotonous: an odd comment from an artist who has always been satisfied with a limited range of imagery, and who has said that his usual emotion while working is boredom. What he really meant, it seems, was that he was discovering the limits of his self-imposed working arena, and he was already beginning to move beyond those limits. It is worth examining how he went about it, for his behavior in the face of a problem tells us a great deal about Johns' methods, and his art. There is his own statement that "I wanted to add something." The expression is typical. He doesn't say he wants to make a break, or to do something else. Rather he wishes to build logically—to add to what is already there. His approach is fundamentally conservative.

In 1958, he painted ALLEY OOP—a comic strip on a color field—using the format of FLAG ON ORANGE FIELD. He said, "I was trying to find some way to apply color in an arbitrary fashion, to incorporate the image within a color field."

Again we see his conservative tendency. Having established the format for FLAG ON ORANGE FIELD, he arbitrarily employs it again for another painting, rather than invent a new composition. Why? Precisely because it is arbitrary. Whatever composition the artist adopted would be arbitrary, and Johns is acutely aware of his choices at every moment. By selecting a previous composition, he visually emphasizes the arbitrary nature of the decision. (He also suggests alternatives, by making us look again at these similarly composed paintings.)

But beyond this, we sense another aspect of Johns' personality and methods. Again and again, we see Johns define his concerns by strictly limiting his own contribution, and by employing arbitrary devices for everything else. If he needs an image, he chooses something in the public domain; if he needs letters, he takes unremarkable stencils not of his making; if he needs color, he tries to find a way to make the selection happen according to some fixed rule he is not responsible for. He never seems to walk the gangplank of personal preference; the decisions in his work can all be explained by some logical, impersonal plan.

Because Johns employs so many mundane, ready-made elements, his work has been widely misunderstood. It is one reason why he was first called anti-art, and why he was first naively considered a Pop Artist. Seen in one perspective, Johns' method is simply his way of expressing a universal creative need—the need to say what your work will *not* be, what it will *not* involve, what limits your creation will exist within.

Creativity is a positive act—making things—and the idea that it is carried out in a negative way first seems illogical. In fact, almost everyone creates this way. Charles Eames tells of a study of creativity among architects; the architects were asked to make a design out of square tiles, from a great range of tiles at their disposal. Afterward one architect proudly announced he had made his entire design from red, white, and blue tiles. Philip Johnson said his design was only black and white. Eero Saarinen then announced he had made *his* design from all white tiles.[29]

One's working methods are often taken to have aesthetic implications. This may or may not be true. But critics who failed to recognize that Johns' working method was a way of setting limits have deduced all sorts of meanings behind his use of ready-made elements. This may be a valid way of looking at the finished work (what way isn't valid?) but it is a clear mistake not to recognize that his working method obliges him to select preexisting imagery in order that his creation will lie elsewhere.[30]

As Johns extended his use of color, he also extended his control of surfaces, and objects attached to the surface, with THREE FLAGS (1958). The idea for this remarkable painting, he says, "came to me all at once—the thought was complete. I have a sketch done on the back of an envelope for it. I was eager to start the picture; I remember I had to wait for the canvas stretchers to be made specially; they had to be bolted to one another. And I remember having a kind of moral conflict about whether to paint the covered portions, because the idea of doing work which will be covered, and is therefore not a part of the necessary information about the picture—that idea conflicts with

ALLEY OOP. 1958. See Plate 33

Sketch for THREE FLAGS. 1958. Charcoal on paper, 12.3 x 24 cm (4^{13}/$_{16}$ x 9^{7}/$_{16}$"). Collection the artist

THREE FLAGS. 1958. See Plate 40

35

the teasing quality of the picture, which suggests that you have done it. I solved it by telling myself that I was doing the painting for myself, and *I* knew that I hadn't painted it." In fact, he painted in the covered areas of the image in gray.

By now, Johns was painting full time; from Rauschenberg he had learned the trick "of only working when you needed money"—he and Rauschenberg designed window displays for Tiffany & Co. and Bonwit Teller and other New York stores, whenever money ran low. Two Johns paintings were first seen in window displays in New York.[31]

But they were seen nowhere else publicly until, at the urging of Allan Kaprow, GREEN TARGET (1955) was included in a group show at the Jewish Museum.[32] There the painting was seen by Leo Castelli.

Trieste-born Leo Castelli was an art collector and self-described playboy who had decided, at the age of 51, to open a gallery.[33] A consummately charming man, he began by selling paintings from his own collection; he also approached some young artists who interested him. In March 1957, soon after the Jewish Museum show, Castelli went to Pearl Street to invite Rauschenberg to show at his gallery. In passing, Castelli mentioned that he had seen a painting by someone with the peculiar name of Jasper Johns,[34] and that he would like to meet the artist. "Well, that's very easy," Rauschenberg said, "he's downstairs."

Rauschenberg then went to Johns' studio to get some ice, and said that Castelli wanted to meet Johns.

"I walked into the studio," Castelli recalled, "and there was this attractive, very shy young man, and all these paintings. It was astonishing, a complete body of work. It was the most incredible thing I've ever seen in my life."

For Johns, who did not want to be associated with any particular group of painters, Castelli was perfect, since his gallery was new and had no specific identity. (Soon enough it had a marked identity, as the gallery of the Pop Artists; by then Castelli was perceived as a brilliant entrepreneur of advanced tastes, or a Machiavellian schemer of subterranean complexity, or both.)

Castelli showed Johns' FLAG (1955) in a group show at his gallery later in 1957, and in 1958 he gave Johns his first one-man show. Here Johns displayed the results of more than three years of sustained effort: his flags, his targets, his numbers and alphabets. Johns became "an overnight sensation,"[35] and was plunged into a critical controversy that continued for several years.

To understand the controversy, one must recall the attitude of the New York art world in the middle 1950s. Abstract Expressionism—that movement which took as its fundamental tenet the necessity of communicating subjective content through an abstract art—was supreme in the city. The importance of Abstract Expressionism was heightened by the recognition that this was the first time in history that an indigenous American art movement had gained international significance.

To say that the New York art world cherished Abstract Expressionism is

GREEN TARGET. 1955. See Plate 12.

an understatement. It was almost impossible to conceive of anything else, to imagine any other premise for painting. As Rauschenberg said of that time, a young painter had "to start every day moving out from Pollock and de Kooning, which is sort of a long way to have to start from."[36] The burden was very heavy.

At the same time, it was true that the second generation of Abstract Expressionist painters often "slavishly imitated"[37] their predecessors. The early shock and excitement of the movement was gone. "As the art market was glutted with the works of de Kooning's admirers, the real achievements of de Kooning and his generation were becoming obscured."[38] There was a sense of waiting for something fresh and new, and newly provocative.

Johns provided the provocation. His assured and finely worked paintings of flags and targets offered an alternative to Abstract Expressionism, and reintroduced representation, the recognizable image, into painting.

Critical opinion on the value of Johns' work, the artist's intention, the implied meaning, and the way the paintings acted on the viewer, was divided and contradictory. There was even disagreement about whether the pictures were well painted: some wrote of "the commanding sensuous presence of . . . Johns' elegant craftsmanship,"[39] which others found "messily painted."[40]

Established artists were not pleased. Leo Steinberg recalls:

> I was interested in the reaction to Jasper Johns of two well-known New York abstract painters: One of them said, "If this is painting, I might as well give up." And the other said, resignedly, "Well, I am still involved with the dream." He, too, felt that an age-old dream of what painting had been, or could be, had been wantonly sacrificed—perhaps by a young man too brash or irreverent to have dreamed yet.[41]

Such comments remind us that if artists are, in McLuhan's phrase, the DEW line, the Distant Early Warning system of a society, they are just as likely to be the Maginot Line, where art is concerned.[42]

Much of the controversy surrounding Johns' first show focused on its popularity. Nearly all the paintings were sold, and many went to influential collectors: Soby, Rockefeller, Johnson, Miller. Alfred Barr bought three paintings, including TARGET WITH FOUR FACES, for the Museum of Modern Art. In the art world, that purchase became a political act,[43] a gesture of confidence and encouragement, that was hotly debated. A year later Ben Heller wrote:

> Johns has been as much a pawn in the current art world game of power politics as the bearer of a new or individual image. As a result of this . . . [he] risks the subtle, swift, and cruel fate befalling one who becomes a fad. . . . He has perhaps suffered as much as gained by his notoriety and success.[44]

The Johns debate continued for nearly half a decade. By then, a new generation of young painters had rejected Abstract Expressionism[45] for post-painterly abstraction and Pop Art—and Johns himself was making

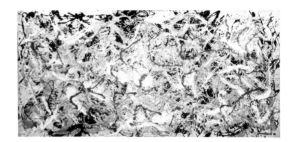

Jackson Pollock. *Number 27*, 1950. Whitney Museum of American Art, New York

FIGURE 5. 1955. See Plate 4

37

pictures distinctly different in imagery and technique from his early flags, targets, and numbers.

Johns denies that his earliest paintings were a reaction to Abstract Expressionism. He says that he didn't know enough, hadn't seen enough, to make such a response. As for the critical consternation, he offers an interesting view: "In those days, the art world was very much smaller than it is now. People had the sense that they knew everything that was going on in the art world in New York. But the fact that nobody had seen these paintings—nobody knew they were being done—increased the surprise when they were finally shown. They were surprising because no one had seen them before."

Was he personally affected by the controversy? "Well, I liked the attention. And I thought it was interesting that other people had a reaction to my work, because prior to that time I had assumed it was mostly of interest only to myself."[46]

But there must have been deeper effects. In 1959, *Time* magazine announced: "Jasper Johns, 29, is the brand-new darling of the art world's bright, brittle avant-garde. A year ago he was practically unknown; since then he has had a sellout show in Manhattan, has exhibited in Paris and Milan, was the only American to win a painting prize at the Carnegie International, and has seen three of his paintings bought for Manhattan's Museum of Modern Art. . . ."[47] One might expect the brand-new darling to be pleased, but the accompanying picture shows a brooding, solemn young man in a coat and tie standing next to one of his paintings. He looks doubtful, and a little suspicious.

Barbara Rose observed that Johns' initial recognition did not bring understanding, and she suggests that much of his early notoriety had less to do with the work itself than with the ease of mass-media dissemination of his simple American images.[48] If Johns found the attention agreeable, he must also have felt it was for all the wrong reasons. That same year, he altered his methods radically. Identified with encaustic, he began to work with oil. Known for targets and flags, he stopped painting them, at least for a while. Recognized as an enigmatic, intellectual artist, he now produced pictures with fewer obvious paradoxes and contradictions.

Thus we are presented with a young artist, having just attained international renown, abandoning the technique, imagery and concerns which made him famous. The result of his transformation—and the cost—are seen clearly in two major paintings of 1959 that can be considered together, FALSE START and JUBILEE.

FALSE START is an explosive picture; it seems to be blowing itself apart, in a kind of pyrotechnic display. Brush strokes are large; color is riotous; composition is not predetermined by mundane imagery. The picture entirely lacks the calm, dignified repose of earlier paintings; on the contrary it appears nervous, risky, unsure of itself. Most striking, FALSE START does not seem to *use* color; it is *about* color, a suspicion confirmed by the presence of JUBILEE, its negative in somber black and white.

The title came accidentally. The artist was sitting in the Cedar Bar, saw a

Jasper Johns at age 29.
Photograph by Ben Martin

racing print titled "False Start," and took that for the name of his own painting. But most observers have sensed a reference to the artist's state of mind, or his feeling while working. Barbara Rose: "A 'False Start' does not occasion a fresh start, but an attempt to retrieve a situation heading out of control."[49] Max Kozloff: "An agitated picture . . . [which] implies an imminent dissolution."[50]

FALSE START. 1959. See Plate 51

The stenciled labels for colors draw attention, since these are often "wrong"—the word GRAY is painted in red letters on a patch of yellow, and so on.

Much dense critical commentary has been devoted to simpleminded contradictions inherent in this mislabeling. (The commentary itself is paradoxical; nearly everyone begins by saying the device is uninteresting, and then discusses it at length.) We may summarize the critical response by saying that most observers found a conflict, or a counterpoint, between the color labels and the splashes of color which they do not really identify. And with the advantage of nearly two decades of hindsight, we can find it peculiar that no one really recognized that Johns—an artist who had already set a course toward increasingly abstract treatment of painting ideas—would quite logically move from images to color, one of the components of images, and that he would deal with color in the same implacably abstract way. At the time, this logical progression was not at all clear.

On first viewing, FALSE START seems to represent a major departure from past pictures.[51] But Johns himself sees no radical break with the past. Two years before, he had become aware of "certain limitations in my work, and I had the need to overcome those, to break with certain habits I had formed, certain procedures I had used. The flags and targets have colors positioned in a predetermined way. I wanted to find a way to apply color so that the color would be determined by some other method." The first paintings to attempt this were FLAG ABOVE WHITE and FLAG ON ORANGE FIELD. The next step was ALLEY OOP. Then came FALSE START.

JUBILEE. 1959. See Plate 52

"It started from an idea about color—the decisions in the painting aren't based on visual sensation primarily. The idea is that the names of color will be scattered about on the surface of the canvas and there will be blotches of color more or less on the same scale, and that one will have all the colors—but all the colors by name, more than by visual sensation."

The interplay of labels and colors "retains the objectness of the painting—I had a need to maintain that quality in the work."

The schematic organization of FALSE START is highlighted by the black-and-white, oddly titled JUBILEE; the pictures were painted one after the other, and they are clearly intended to be considered together. The idea of such paired images is itself a conception of great importance to Johns' later work. In succeeding years he returned again and again to the double image, the mirror image, until it finally became central to all his work.

But with JUBILEE, there is at least the suspicion of something more bizarre—not merely that the painting relates to its colored twin, but that it may have come from direct experience.

Johns always describes himself with a peculiar flat accuracy. He insists he

FALSE START (detail). 1959. See Plate 51

is a poor colorist, with little ability to discriminate between colors he sees. He says he is worse at this than the average person. One is tempted to take him at his word. Then he reports this anecdote: "I was working on a colored numbers painting. When I worked on it for longer than a minute, the entire painting would turn gray to me. I couldn't see any of the colors, and I would have to stop."

For JUBILEE, this is a highly suggestive anecdote; and it invites speculation for the entire body of Johns' work, so often characterized by muted grays. In addition, it requires one to look again at his most colorful work—the prints of the FIGURES IN COLOR (1968–69), for example—to see if they can be explained as the work of someone who is a poor colorist.

But the experience of seeing a painting turn gray before his eyes must have made work difficult; puzzled, "I mentioned this to Duchamp. He said, 'Perhaps you have a physiological need. . . .' " In the end, that seems as good an explanation as any.

Marcel Duchamp.
Photograph by Fred McDarrah

Johns met Marcel Duchamp in 1959.[52] The French painter was brought to his studio by the critic Nicolas Calas. Johns never knew Duchamp well, or saw him often. Mostly he saw him with John Cage, who studied chess with Duchamp. Nevertheless Marcel Duchamp is usually considered a major influence on Johns' work and ideas.

After one's youth, an "influence" really implies an underlying congruity of thought. Jasper Johns at 29, a newly successful and active painter, had much in common with Marcel Duchamp, then 72, an artist who had not worked publicly for many years.[53] Both were highly intellectual, highly sensual artists; both worked through negation, producing teasing, cryptic, hide-and-seek creations; both employed ready-made elements in their work; both concerned themselves with the interplay of thought and language, chance and intent, representation and perception. Personally there were similarities as well. Both men were private people with a distinctive sense of humor; and both were often perceived as detached, austere, and cold.

With so much in common, it is not surprising that they have fared similarly at the hands of art history. Duchamp is usually considered the father of Dada, the anti-art movement of the 1920s. In his first public exposure, Johns was perceived as "neo-Dada" in his efforts and intentions. It was some time before the real difference in their attitudes and work became clear.

Years later, Johns wrote that Duchamp's work moved "into a field where language, thought and vision act upon one another. There it changed form through a complex interplay of new mental and physical materials. . . ."[54] It is not a bad description of Johns' own concerns, and an interesting way to look at a fascinating picture of 1959, DEVICE CIRCLE.

DEVICE CIRCLE seems to bridge the new and the old. It is done in the familiar medium of encaustic, and its circular enclosure echoes the targets. We can see how the circle was made—the "device" is left attached to the canvas. But what the circle encloses is problematical; inside and outside are not distinct; we sense the artist who could once be comfortably labeled "hermetic" bursting out of his self-imposed borders.

In Johns' own view of the painting, the idea of boundaries is significant. "In my earlier pictures, the gestures [of painting] have to conform to the boundaries. That's the only thing they have to do, stay within the lines. But in the paintings of this time, there was an attempt to find a way that gestures would make up an image: the gestures would determine the boundaries."

As for the device, it had the arbitrary impersonal quality so important to Johns' work: "I was trying to find something to do that would determine a large part of the nature of the work."

Max Kozloff:

> The "device circle". . . is not an emblem, like the flag, or a system, like the numbers and alphabets, or a "subject," like the maps. . . . *Device Circle* can be thought of as a *False Start* ground upon which a circle was to be drawn. Rather than a string stretched across from the center in order to establish the figure, Johns employs a stick for his compass, and then, the job done, leaves it attached to the surface. The circle corrals the denser chromatic splutters—red, white, yellow, and blue—into the center, where they are physically constrained, if not formally harmonized, by the *tondo* shape. There is, then, an uneasy compromise between the interior and exterior of the circle. . . . And almost painful is the contrast between the easily made and perfect arc and the labored, newspaper-clotted façade.[55]

The uneasy compromise between interior and exterior must have characterized the artist's personal life in those days. One senses it in the young man standing diffidently beside the TARGET WITH FOUR FACES, almost as if he does not want to be associated with his own work. But the work always reflects the inner state of the artist, even if he explicitly denies any correlation between his feelings and his creations.

When Johns says, "I didn't want my work to be an exposure of my feelings," he is really divorcing himself from the tenets of Abstract Expressionism, where the goal of the work, the point of the painting, was some statement of subjective emotion. Johns never had this goal. To that extent his statement is literally correct.

But it is impossible for anyone to create out of purely intellectual, unemotional impulses. I doubt such impulses exist, in the first place; but even if they did, the act of creation, extending over time, would incorporate other elements which must be defined as emotional.

What is the young man in the photograph thinking? He tells us—in a sense—in a sculpture of 1959, THE CRITIC SMILES. This is clearly a response to public attention; one cannot imagine it being made a few years before by the patient creator of flags and targets that nobody saw. This is a reaction to *being seen.*

When Johns first received public attention, he refused to be drawn into a critical dialogue. In *Newsweek* in 1958 he said, "I have no ideas about what the paintings imply about the world. I don't think that's a painter's business. He just paints paintings without a conscious reason."[56] Nothing could be

DEVICE CIRCLE. 1959. See Plate 46

41

THE CRITIC SMILES. 1959. See Plate 62

Picasso. *Baboon and Young* (detail). 1951.
The Museum of Modern Art, New York.
Mrs. Simon Guggenheim Fund

further from Johns' actual views about work; he is a highly self-conscious painter. But one cannot fault him for refusing to speak. He was at this time getting his first taste of what the established art world was really about. Years later he said, "The art world works on many levels. Most of them are not publicly acknowledged." Johns must have had a lot to absorb; and his response was THE CRITIC SMILES.

THE CRITIC SMILES operates as a kind of illusion, in the same way as Picasso's *Baboon and Young* (1951); it exemplifies Johns' dictum that "you can see more than one thing at a time"; and it demonstrates a reversal of the acted and the acted-upon, the teeth and the bristles.

Recently he said about it: "I had the idea that in society the approval of the critic was a kind of cleansing police action. When the critic smiles it's a lopsided smile with hidden meanings. And of course a smile involves baring the teeth. The critic is keeping a certain order, which is why it is like a police function. The handle has the word 'copper' on it, which I associate with police. I imagined the sculpture to be done in various metals—base lead, handle silver, teeth gold."

The puns suggested by his description should not obscure another aspect, his interest in working with different materials. Johns has always strived to extend his technical facility. This passive and retiring man, who ordinarily works slowly and thoughtfully, is positively aggressive in his assault on new technical challenges. New techniques never intimidate him; he has gone into lithography, serigraphy, etching, and offset printing with a boldness that has astonished—and even frightened—those around him. In part this must reflect self-confidence: from the beginning of his career, Johns has been recognized as an artist with an awesome technical facility. But beyond that, I suspect that this most analytical of artists has a special need to engage his conscious mind; he uses demanding technical problems to free his unconscious from the constraints of thought.[57] If this supposition is correct, then pure technical challenges are an essential requirement for him to work—and certainly his creations are most spontaneous during the period of his first exposure to a new medium; once he has mastered the technique, his work becomes more intricate, and convoluted.

There seems to be a natural cycle of about four years between Johns' first entry into a medium, and his subsequent need to do something else.[58] Thus he began serious painting in 1954; in 1958 he made his first sculptures—ordinary objects, flashlights, and light bulbs.

If we ignore the theme of illumination, we find his initial interest was again provoked by materials—the idea of combining glass and some other substance into a single object. He was also aware of playing on the confusion of the handmade object, and the ready-made object. FLASHLIGHT I (1958), his first, is sculp-metal over an actual store-bought flashlight; later flashlights were made from scratch in papier-mâché, and in plaster.

The confusion of illusive art and concrete object, always a theme in his painting, was carried to a kind of logical extreme with his famous 1960 sculpture of ale cans, PAINTED BRONZE.

It began with a chance remark. "Somebody told me that Bill de Kooning said [of Leo Castelli] that you could give that son of a bitch two beer cans and he could sell them. I thought, what a wonderful idea for a sculpture." He made it soon after, two ale cans ("I was drinking ale at the time"). They were made in plaster of paris, in a complicated way. "Parts were done by casting, parts by building up from scratch, parts by molding, breaking, and then restoring. I was deliberately making it difficult to tell how it was made." The sculpture was then cast in bronze, reworked when it came back from the foundry, and finally painted.

Soon after, he did the sculpture PAINTED BRONZE (1960), the Savarin can with brushes. "The idea for the ale cans was like a present. I felt I should already have known to do it as a sculpture: it had the right scale, it was already there—all I had to do was look over and see it, and then do it. Doing the ale cans made me see other things around me, so I did the Savarin Can. I think what interested me was the coffee can used to hold turpentine for brushes—the idea of one thing mixed with another for a purpose."

PAINTED BRONZE. 1960. See Plate 67

In 1960, he began work in still another medium, lithography. Tatyana Grosman, who had started Universal Limited Art Editions in her house at West Islip, Long Island, in 1957, wrote Johns a letter inviting him to work there. He sent her a card from South Carolina, saying that he would come when he was next in New York. Eventually an appointment was set.

Mrs. Grosman recalls, "I was sitting in the living room waiting for Jasper, and suddenly very fast a young man walks in, and I think, what does he want? I think perhaps he is lost, or wanting directions. I didn't want to be disturbed, because I was waiting for Jasper. . . . I didn't understand that he *was* Jasper." After their first meeting, she arranged for two lithograph stones to be taken to his studio in New York, for him to work on.

Succeeding years have seen an enormous resurgence in fine-art printing, attributable partly to Mrs. Grosman's tactful persistence, and partly to June Wayne's Ford Foundation-sponsored Tamarind Workshop in Los Angeles and its offspring, including Gemini G.E.L. in the same city, started by Ken Tyler. It is difficult, now, to imagine how peculiar a lithograph stone—and the very idea of making prints—seemed to American artists in the 1960s. Rauschenberg's view was typical: he thought the latter part of the twentieth century was no time to start writing on rocks. But Rauschenberg, who himself became a master of the medium, finally spoke eloquently of it, referring to the "skin of the stone."

To an outsider, fine-art lithography is a crazy world,[59] centered around the stone—the limestone slab, incredibly heavy, polished to a silky sheen which does, in fact, resemble skin. The stones are extremely valuable; all the best stones came from one quarry in Bavaria, now exhausted. Within a lithography shop, each stone has a personality. Some are easy, some are hard; some resist an impression, some welcome it; some take crayon well, others take a wash well; some become a favorite of one artist or another, and are reserved for that particular artist, who may do several prints on the same stone—which is ground and polished between prints—until the artist and

PAINTED BRONZE. 1960. See Plate 68

43

the printers all come to know a particular stone as if it were a member of their family.

Printers worry over their stones; they visit them in the middle of the night; they talk about them as if they were individuals, and not chunks of inanimate matter. Contrasting with this anthropomorphic tendency is a highly technological craft, which has developed as printing has moved away from simple lithography. The use of zinc and aluminum plates, photosensitive techniques, combined printing and silkscreening, and most recently the introduction of the offset press, have added to the complexity.

The printmaking process is very far from the life of the solitary painter, alone with his brushes, his canvas, and his thoughts. For a painter, lithography demands not only a whole new range of techniques—on a stone, for example, everything must be drawn backward, and in only one color at a time—but an entirely different method of working. Printmaking is a collaborative process, an interaction between the artist, the stone, the plates, and the printers who ink the image and transfer it to paper. The process is so complete that it takes on a life of its own which no single person controls. There is nothing solitary about it.

Finally, we might note that in printmaking, the flatness of the image is an inherent feature of the work. One can do almost anything in printing except suggest the kind of surface that is easily created in painting; prints are flat; they are printed on paper; and that, as they say, is that.

Johns began printmaking by trying to complicate the lithography process as much as possible.

"I left the stones with Jasper," Mrs. Grosman recalls, "and after a time he said I could come to collect them. There were two: a target and a zero. The target was all right, but the other one! He explained that the zero had to be printed, and then the drawing partially erased, and a numeral one printed, and then that would be erased. . . . I didn't know if it was even possible to make these changes, but I said we would try. The stones were brought down to the car by Jasper and another young man. He was funny; he said, 'That's art, to carry something so heavy.' That was the first time I met Rauschenberg."

The zero stone eventually became the extraordinary series of prints, 0–9 (1960–63). Johns recalls that he began drawing on the stone as a kind of test of the medium. He drew all the numbers zero through nine at the top in two rows, and then, because there was more space below, he drew a large zero. But he felt that this print, alone, "was a little peculiar." So he conceived the idea of doing a series of ten prints, all based on this single stone, which would be worked again and again to create a full series of numbers. This project was not carried out for two years, because Mrs. Grosman was looking for the proper paper to print it on.

When it was finally printed, there were actually three series of ten prints. One series was printed in gray on eggshell paper; a second was printed in black on off-white paper; a third was printed in color on white paper.[60] This means that each stone was printed in three different ways, then re-drawn,

Figure 0 from 0–9. 1960–63. Lithograph, 52.1 x 40 cm (20½ x 15¾"). Published by ULAE

44

printed again, and so on. "As a result of Johns' incredibly skillful drawing and the transparency of the lithographic inks, the series is not only a bravura demonstration of the possibilities of the medium but a subtle essay on change, seen in the visual symbols of change."[61]

The first lithograph to be printed and released was the much simpler TARGET (1960). It is probably true that in any extension into a new medium, there is a tendency to revert to past familiar themes in order to isolate what is new; a kind of regression accompanies growth. Thus in 1960 Johns painted PAINTING WITH TWO BALLS, but his lithographs referred to much older imagery; the target, coat hanger, and numerals 0 through 9. This delay between painting and print continued for a time; he made a print, PAINTING WITH TWO BALLS I, in 1962, and his magnificent ALE CANS in 1964. Eventually the order was reversed; the print DECOY (1971) actually preceded the painting of the same name (for illustration, see page 59).

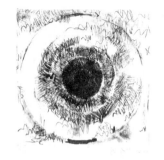

TARGET. 1960. See Plate 69

DECOY is enormously complex, very different from the first printed TARGET, which in scale and technique suggests a conté crayon drawing made directly on the stone. Aside from its historical importance, this TARGET is interesting because it is the clearest suggestion we have that a target can be compared to the pupil of an eye. James Thurber:

> The instructor, noting my activity, came back from an adjoining desk, a smile on his lips and his eyebrows high in hope. He looked at my cell drawing. "What's that?" he demanded, with a hint of a squeal in his voice. "That's what I saw," I said. . . . "That's your eye!" he shouted. "You've fixed the lens so that it reflects! You've drawn your eye!"[62]

Although Johns' first lithograph was much like a drawing, he was quick to exploit the unique potential of the medium. In the same year, 1960, he did FLAG I, II, and III, a series of transformed images that provides a very good idea of what he is about—from the initial flag, in tusche, printed black on white; to the second state, in which the stone is changed by the addition of lines of wash and crayon, giving a more "scribbled" appearance, then printed in white on kraft paper; to the third state, in which the stone is again changed by a pattern of scratches which furthers the idea of the crayon lines. All together these images exemplify the Johns dictum, "Take an object/Do something to it/Do something else to it."[63]

ALE CANS. 1964. See Plate 122

Within five years, Johns was an acknowledged master of printmaking. By the end of the decade, he had made more than 120 prints. Much of his work during the late 1960s concerned prints—so much, in fact, that there were dark rumors that Jasper Johns was finished, burned out, as a painter.

There were no such rumors in 1961, a year of further confident growth. The large MAP represents an addition to his repertoire of imagery. The previous year, Rauschenberg had given Johns a schematic American map of the sort used in a school notebook, and Johns had painted over it; he used those proportions to paint the larger map.[64]

Paint drips are a prominent feature in this MAP; they are much more

MAP. 1960. Encaustic on paper on canvas, 20.3 x 27.9 cm (8 x 11"). Collection Robert Rauschenberg

MAP. 1961. See Plate 74

striking than in previous paintings, and provide a good reason to discuss the role of accident in the creation of his work. In ordinary life, such drips usually imply a mistake, or sloppy indifference. And there is a persistent theme in modern art, a theme of using chance events, which the viewing public has always mistrusted.

Duchamp, who employed chance in his working method, once said, "Your chance is not the same as my chance. . . ."[65] He meant that the outcome of probability events is actually an expression of the artist's subconscious. This idea that you control what you do not control may at first seem surprising. In fact it is widely held. Suzuki on swordfighting:

> Some may ask: How can the sword which implements the will to kill work out its function by itself without the willer's directive behind it? What originality, what creative work, can an inanimate mechanical tool be made to carry out all by itself? When a tool performs whatever function it is made to perform, how can we say it has achieved something original?
>
> The point is: When the sword is . . . held by the swordsman whose spiritual attainment is such that he holds it as though not holding it, it is identified with the man himself, it acquires a soul, it moves with all the subtleties which have been imbedded in him as a swordsman. The man . . . is not conscious of using the sword; both man and sword turn into instruments in the hands, as it were, of the unconscious, and it is this unconscious that achieves wonders of creativity.[66]

Johns' own view is not quite so no-minded: "There are no accidents in my work. It sometimes happens that something unexpected occurs—the paint may run—but then I see that it has happened, and I have the choice to paint it again or not. And if I don't, then the appearance of that element in the painting is no accident."

Some observers are put off by ideas like these. The artist does not seem to be struggling to bring forth some preexisting vision, but rather is engaged in a process where the outcome may or may not conform to the initial idea, and where accidents along the way are incorporated. The idea of following a process in artistic creation makes people uneasy; the idea of a struggle—birth pangs—is much more acceptable.

Thus the cliché that the artist is never satisfied with his work, that it never turns out to be what he "had in mind." But why not? The usual explanation assumes that imagination has a richness beyond what the fingers can actually perform, so disappointment inevitably follows. Much has been written about the eternal striving of the artist to reproduce the wondrous visions in his brain.

In fact, one can argue that human imagination is far paler than its concrete manifestations. Certainly imagination is often simply wrong. There is a fine example of this in Johns' own work. In 1958, he did a drawing, COAT HANGER, and a painting the following year. The drawing shows the coat hanger bar parallel to the bottom of the picture. A thoughtful viewer will sense that something is wrong, and something is—coat hangers don't hang that way, except in the imagination, which tends to idealize, to tidy things up. Johns was surprised to discover his error, when he actually executed the painting with a real coat hanger.

Similarly, there is often a disparity between the idea, and the imagined way of carrying it out. In PAINTING WITH TWO BALLS, Johns envisioned spheres wedged between horizontal panels of a three-paneled painting. He intended to make the painting by bolting the canvases together and then pushing the balls into the position he wanted. He was surprised to find this didn't work: the canvas wrinkled badly. To create the effect he had imagined, he was obliged to take an unforeseen step—the construction of two special curved canvas stretchers.[67]

A great many surprises occur while making something, and if you live with those surprises long enough, they begin to seem like an ordinary feature of working. They cease to be remarkable; they are like the swells that rock a boat; you begin to compensate for them, to ride them, to go along with them. Soon there is little distinction between what you intended and what you are doing. Everyone's work is the outcome of a thousand apparently accidental events that are permitted—or not permitted—to enter the final work.

Seen in this way, creation is *only* a process, and the idea has no significance beyond the fact that it sets the process in motion. The relationship between the idea and the final product is always doubtful. Things change, and may even become inverted. As psychologist Jerome Bruner says, "You are more likely to act yourself into feeling than to feel yourself into action."[68] Johns himself echoes the idea: "Sometimes I see it and then paint it. Other times I paint it and then see it."[69]

Returning to the 1961 MAP, with all its drips, we can imagine that the paint started to drip, and the artist liked it, left it, and perhaps even encouraged it. In any case, it is so prominent a feature of the painting—and it is less evident in the other maps[70]—that it cannot be considered accidental.

These questions stand alongside another debate among artists themselves about what is important in a created work. Borges wrote: "The composition of vast books is a laborious and impoverishing extravagance. To go on for five hundred pages developing an idea whose perfect oral exposition is possible in a few minutes! A better course of procedure is to pretend that these books already exist, and then to offer a résumé, a commentary."[71]

In the same way, Marcel Duchamp said that he was interested only in the idea of a painting, and not in the surrounding vehicle of its transmission. This was one difficulty Johns had with Duchamp's thought; Johns felt that it was impossible to distinguish between the idea and the creation—after all, when the work was done, the idea was the painting.[72] There could be no difference. On the most simplistic level, one could say that the melody was not the symphony.[73]

In the work of 1961, we see an increasingly personal reference in the titles: BY THE SEA, GOOD TIME CHARLEY, IN MEMORY OF MY FEELINGS—FRANK O'HARA. This is a departure from the coldly descriptive, literal titles that

COAT HANGER. 1958. See Plate 34

COAT HANGER. 1959. Encaustic on canvas with objects, 70.5 x 53.9 cm (27¾ x 21¼"). Private collection

The Critic Sees. 1964. Sculp-metal on plaster with glass, 8.2 x 15.8 x 5.4 cm (3¼ x 6¼ x 2⅛″). Collection the artist

No. 1961. See Plate 80

Johns first gave his work, and it may reflect Duchamp's influence. "I like what Duchamp said, that a title should be like another color to the work."

There was a new influence in this period, the philosopher Ludwig Wittgenstein, whom Johns read avidly during the early 1960s. (Interestingly, he dates his exposure to Wittgenstein from the painting FOOL'S HOUSE.) As with Duchamp, one senses a kindred spirit, for Wittgenstein is preoccupied with language, meaning, measurement, structured relationships, and the interpretation of visual information.

This latter is important in a 1961 sculpture, THE CRITIC SEES. It was created in response to an experience: "I was hanging a show of sculpture and drawings, and a critic came in and started asking me what things were. He paid no attention to what I said. He said what do you call these? and I said sculpture. He said why do you call them sculpture when they're just casts. I said they weren't casts, that some had been made from scratch, and others had been casts that were broken and reworked. He said yes, they're casts, not sculpture. It went on like that."

Like the earlier THE CRITIC SMILES, this piece functions partly as an optical trick, partly as an implied comment about the art world, and partly as a more general statement about the nature of perception. There is a clear suggestion that seeing and talking are related, and perhaps even equated;[74] there is also the idea that what is visually interesting provokes speech. For a South Carolinian who spent most of his youth not far from Charleston, a pun on the phrase "Oh, say, can you see?" has also been proposed.

Most commentary has focused on the raised image, ignoring the bricklike structure of the sculpture as a whole. It is impossible to miss the sense of imprisonment, of being boxed in, that the piece implies. THE CRITIC SEES is funny, but not very optimistic.

Neither is a painting from that year, a kind of penultimate statement of negation, No. On a somber surface, a screw-eye suspends a wire which goes into the canvas, then re-emerges to dangle the metal letters: NO. The letters stand away from a painted NO underneath. When illuminated, the metal casts one, or sometimes two shadow NOs on the painted surface. It is a picture full of NO.

About this time, Johns began to turn his back on the routine of the New York art world. He was sufficiently established that he was no longer obliged to have an annual show; he stopped having them. He lived only part of the year in New York; the rest of the time he spent at a house in Edisto Beach, South Carolina.

Increasingly, his work turned inward upon itself, becoming more self-referential, more difficult, more disturbing. Rose refers to "the artist's own string of self-accusations: *Liar; Good Time Charley; Fool's House.*"[75] Kozloff says, "Unavoidable is the impression of a world gone awry, tumultuously churning up one's experience. . . .These works. . .tend to convey an underlying desperation."[76]

Whether that desperation was in the mind of the artist or the critic struggling to make sense of the new paintings, it is true that the paintings of 1961–64 seem peculiarly resistant to interpretation.

Some general comments can be made. The paintings tend to be simply composed into horizontal or vertical segments, either because they are made of several canvas panels, or because some hanging object forms a division. There is a progression, a conservation tendency, in composition and imagery. Thus, the triple horizontal RED YELLOW BLUE panels which first appear in OUT THE WINDOW (1959)—where they are reminiscent of FALSE START—reappear in the single canvas of OUT THE WINDOW NUMBER 2 (1962), as well as in BY THE SEA (1961), DIVER (1962), PASSAGE (1962), PERISCOPE (HART CRANE) (1963), LAND'S END (1963), and WATCHMAN (1964). This reworking of a compositional idea makes the horizontal RED YELLOW BLUE a kind of "flag" which, once conceived, is endlessly renewed and shown in different ways.[77]

Increasingly, the artist leaves his literal impression in the picture—his hands and feet, sometimes his whole arm, and finally his photographic image, printed in a souvenir plate.[78] In this regard, a series of drawings, STUDIES FOR SKIN I–IV (1962), is important. They are beautiful, ghostly images, made by pressing oiled skin to paper, then rubbing charcoal over the oil residue. But they were done for a specific reason.

In 1962 Johns had the idea of casting an entire head, then making a thin rubber mask from the cast and, cutting the rubber, placing it flat on a surface, and casting the entire work in bronze. The result would be a "map" of skin, but the question remained of how to cut the rubber skin and lay it out. For this reason the studies were done. (The piece was not completed.)[79]

Perhaps the most striking feature about Johns' paintings from 1961–64 is his use of attached or hanging household objects—kitchen utensils, cups, brooms—or artist's devices—rulers, paintbrushes, rags, small hinged canvases. These hanging objects are usually named, but their presence is disturbing and troublesome.

The combination of elements, canvas panels, painted surfaces, imprints, and objects reminds one of anthropologist Edmund Carpenter's assessment of tribal art:

> It's full of abrupt encounters—sudden interfaces, then emptiness. When you have interface & emptiness . . . surfaces & events collide & grind against each other, creating new forms, much as the action of dialogue creates new insights. It's the world of all-at-onceness where things hit each other but where there are no connections.[80]

Certainly, the connections in these paintings are doubtful. The pictures suggest less and less some relationship to the outside world, the world of the spectator, and more and more some set of relationships within their own boundaries. Barbara Rose put it nicely: "Their meanings, if decipherable, lie entirely within the world created on canvas or paper. Within this world, not the identity of the objects, but the nature of their relationships counts."[81]

Johns himself has confirmed this. For example, of ZONE he said, "The idea was the interaction of two areas, one encaustic, one oil." And at least

OUT THE WINDOW. 1959. See Plate 56

OUT THE WINDOW NUMBER 2. 1962.
See Plate 102

49

ZONE. 1962. See Plate 101

PERISCOPE (HART CRANE). 1963. See Plate 105

obliquely, he has confirmed the critics' feelings of his desperation. LAND'S END, he said, was given that title "because I had the sense of arriving at a point where there was no place to stand." It is a point where nothing is certain anymore, where everything is "confused by thought," and where, whatever you decide about a painting, you can find the reverse within the same canvas borders.

No can be taken as the beginning of this particularly troublesome group of paintings. Johns said of this picture: "Small differences are important. Or if they are not important, they could be seen as important to someone who devoted himself to that kind of thing." In fact, the painting combines a great many materials—canvas, collage, wax, wood, lead, galvanized wire, steel, sculp-metal—in ways that are not obvious. The title pun on "know" and the variety of materials, whether perceived or not, remind one of Virchow's classic comment, "We see what we know."[82]

The problems of perception—of seeing what we know, and knowing what we see—are emphasized by the titles, which tend to have a geographical reference, or a statement of the observer's position: BY THE SEA, LAND'S END, OUT THE WINDOW, PERISCOPE (HART CRANE). This latter title is taken from a passage in Crane's poem "Cape Hatteras":

. . . while time clears
Our lenses, lifts a focus, resurrects
A periscope to glimpse what joys or pain
Our eyes can share or answer—then deflects
Us, shunting to a labyrinth submersed
Where each sees only his dim past reversed. . .[83]

A submersed labyrinth is not a bad description of these paintings, taken as a group. They have the hidden undercurrents, the redundancy, the apparently pointless juxtapositions of a dream. That they are more difficult than earlier paintings may be a normal progression. Jung said: "Initial dreams are often amazingly lucid and clear-cut. But as the work of analysis progresses, the dreams tend to lose their clarity. . . . As a rule, dreams get more and more opaque and blurred soon after the beginning of the treatment, and this makes the interpretation increasingly difficult."[84] Whether we choose to view these paintings as a sequence of dreams, or whether we regard them as an artist progressively painting himself into a corner, we must acknowledge that the idea of genuinely self-referential art, of work that asks you to decide about it solely on the basis of what is presented to you, is extremely difficult. It is difficult to create, and difficult to look at.

In one sense it is an absolutely logical next step for a painter whose first interest lay partly in depriving his picture of context, of outside associations. An American flag is painted by Johns for reasons having little to do with that particular image. But the viewer inevitably brings to the work some associations to the flag. To eradicate those associations, to eliminate any context other than what the painter himself allows, is not so easily done. Pure abstraction is no solution: even Polonius can see figures in clouds; in that sense, the process of "reading in" is made easier by abstraction. Johns' solution is to use familiar objects, cups and forks, for which the viewer has so many associations that the object becomes, in a sense, meaningless.

If self-referential art is difficult, it is also dangerous. Carried much further, Johns would have inevitably declined into either immobility, total paralysis—or the indecipherable internal references of schizophrenia. There had to be a break, and it came in 1964, with a trip to Hawaii and Japan. He and his friends John Cage and Lois Long spent a month on Oahu, where Johns began sketches for three important paintings: WATCHMAN, SOUVENIR, and ACCORDING TO WHAT. En route they had stopped in San Francisco, where Cage's music was performed in a series of concerts honoring the musician David Tudor at the Tape Music Center. During a performance, Johns saw a spot of light moving over the ceiling of the darkened hall. He eventually determined that this was coming from a woman's compact mirror. The light, mirror, and reflected spot made him think, "That will be in my next painting."

SOUVENIR. 1964. See Plate 116

In SOUVENIR,[85] a flashlight shines onto a bicycle mirror in a corner of the canvas, and this light is reflected onto a plate—similar to the cheap souvenir plates found the world over—which contains the artist's photograph, and the words RED YELLOW BLUE around the perimeter. The canvas itself is dark, a heavily worked encaustic surface. Johns thought of the painting as a souvenir of Japan. It is an image of indirection as well; the flashlight, an old Johns' object, now illuminates the artist's replica of himself, by bouncing its light all over the painting. (The fact that this system does not work very well—a much-discussed feature of the picture—is another discovery of working. Johns expected that the light would shine nicely onto the plate, but it just didn't turn out that way.)

It can be taken as a sort of metaphor for how Johns thinks of his work: the past is strongly evident, but in a disguised or altered form; the artist has left his own image, but it is illuminated indirectly. All these events take place around the borders of the canvas surface; they are distractions which carry us away from any examination of that surface, which is dim and forbidding.

WATCHMAN has aroused interest in part because of notes Johns published. These notes seem to suggest an explanation, or a further illumination, of the images:

The watchman falls "into" the "trap" of looking. The "spy" is a different person. "Looking" is and is not "eating" and "being eaten." (Cézanne?—each object reflecting the other.) That is, there is continuity of some sort among the watchman, the space, the objects. The spy must be ready to "move," must be aware of his entrances and exits. The watchman leaves his job & takes away no information. The spy must remember and must remember himself and his remembering. The spy designs himself to be overlooked. The watchman "serves" as a warning. Will the spy and the watchman ever meet? In a painting named SPY, will he be present? The spy stations himself to observe the watchman. If the spy is a foreign object, why is the eye not irritated? Is he invisible? When the spy irritates, we try to remove him. "Not spying, just looking"—Watchman.[86]

WATCHMAN. 1964. See Plate 118

51

A person's notes are not ordinarily written to be read by others; the stream of consciousness in the passage above is less helpful than it first appears to be. Attempts to make detailed connections between the notes and the painted images have come to a dead end.[87]

The notes suggest that this is a picture about looking. They identify the cast of the leg and chair,[88] inverted in one corner; that is the watchman (falling into the trap of looking?). The rest of the painting at first suggests a typical Johnsian division into horizontal segments labeled RED YELLOW BLUE. The left side is relatively colorless; the primary colors appear on the right. At the bottom there is a smear of paint which makes a gray scale. The smearing "device" is left there, propped against a ball. The paint strokes emanating from the seated figure strike out and disrupt the loose organization of the painting as a whole. We are told "there is continuity of some sort among the watchman, the space, the objects." What sort of continuity? Evidently, the raw materials of perception are exposed here—words and letters, gray scale, primary colors, casts, real objects—but if we are to "see" it all, we are immediately trapped into asking questions, into bringing our intellect to bear. Perception is not passive, but active; a process of interpretation and "digestion." And even to be given the raw materials, the basic blocks of vision, is also to be provided with food for thought.

It may be that Johns got from Duchamp the idea of allowing notes to reflect on a painting, for Duchamp's notes for his *Green Box* can be thought of as an important part of the work itself. Johns was, to some degree, caught up with Duchamp during these years. He had several dreams about him which were memorable. One was: "I dreamed there was a party, with a lot of people. Marcel was lying flat on a table and I saw him from his feet, like that painting. The party went on in a very lively way but Marcel did not move. Finally someone began tapping him on the leg, and saying 'There's something wrong with Marcel, there's something wrong with Marcel.' By then I had moved up to his head, so I saw him from a different perspective. This person kept saying, 'There's something wrong with Marcel.' Then Marcel sat up, very abruptly, and said something extremely funny, and everyone laughed."

This dream, a wake for Marcel Duchamp who is not awake, proposes that there is something wrong with Duchamp, which is corrected when Johns sees him from a different perspective. This different perspective on Duchamp appears in the 1964 painting, ACCORDING TO WHAT.

It is the largest, most ambitious painting Johns had made until that time. In all sorts of ways, it suggests a catalog, and a summary. It is a compendium of past Johnsian elements—the inverted chair and cast leg of WATCHMAN, the hinged canvases of PORTRAIT—VIOLA FARBER and SLOW FIELD, the spectrum letters of the FIELD paintings, the bent coat hangers of EVIAN, the spoon of GRAY PAINTING WITH SPOON, the primary color blocks of many paintings, the gray scale of DIVER. And this picture shows a typically simple underlying composition of vertical canvas panels, crossed by a band of silkscreened newsprint. Once again, the picture seems to suggest a complex internal world in which the parts are related to one another, according to . . . what?

Andrea Mantegna. *Dead Christ*. After 1466. Brera Gallery, Milan

EVIAN. 1964. Oil on canvas with objects, 174 x 127 cm (68½ x 50"). Private collection.

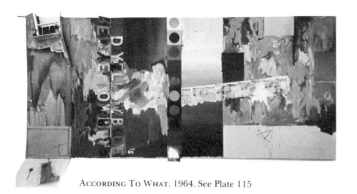

Marcel Duchamp. *Tu m'*. 1918. Yale University Art Gallery, New Haven.
Gift from the Estate of Katherine S. Dreier

ACCORDING TO WHAT. 1964. See Plate 115

Duchamp's profile appears on the inside of the hinged canvas, lower left, and ACCORDING TO WHAT can be considered a response to Duchamp's large painting *Tu m'*. Barbara Rose observes that both paintings catalog "the varieties of representation": both contain real objects, both have the shadows of objects, both contain painted images, and both show representations in perspective. Rose suggests that Johns adds two more varieties: reproduction, with the silkscreened swath of newsprint, and replication ("A three-dimensional cast of a human leg . . . is essentially a replica of a leg . . .").[89]

For Johns, this representational index is directly turned to questions of perception. The brushy colored area in the upper right contrasts with the primary color blocks that represent its origins, the painter's starting point; the gray scale is a continuous spectrum while the adjacent color circles show the discontinuous effects of addition and subtraction in typical Johnsian fashion (yellow plus blue makes green; green minus yellow makes blue; blue plus red makes purple; and so on). These colored circles are reminiscent of the color scales used in printing, and indeed Johns uses color scales at the borders of later paintings. We are also reminded of Cage's statement that Duchamp showed the value of addition, with his moustache on Leonardo's *Mona Lisa;* that Rauschenberg showed the usefulness of subtraction, with the erased de Kooning drawing; and, Cage concluded, Johns was likely to discover the usefulness of trigonometry.[90] In Johns' work that has often meant the interaction of intellectual constructs and verbal concepts with visual material, here represented by the color spectrum RED YELLOW BLUE, not painted, like the gray scale, but written (in appropriate colors) and, in fact, made three-dimensional with attached hinged letters. The fact that the letters are often bent or warped adds another level of complexity as does the cast, which is shown reversed, so that we see the "other side" of something that does not logically have another side. Or put another way, the representation has features of its own that do not correspond to the referent; Johns emphasizes these. "Blue" is a word referring to a color; its referent is a concept that cannot be said to be bendable, but Johns has bent *his* BLUE. And while a human leg has an anatomical interior filled with structures, it has no "inside" of the sort we are shown. Only a cast has an inside.[91]

Finally, we might note that both Johns' painting and Duchamp's represent their creators' final words on a subject. For Duchamp, *Tu m'* was literally the final work; he never made another painting. For Johns, AC-

CORDING TO WHAT was merely the point of another redefinition of himself and his past, of the sort he had already done twice, and would do twice again.

Johns' self-revisions have been variously received. In the early 1960s, he was called "one of America's liveliest and most original younger artists,"[92] and "the white, or gray, hope of American painting."[93] In 1963 *Newsweek* magazine said "Jasper Johns at 32 is probably the most influential younger painter in the world. He has produced surprise after surprise. . . ."[94]

There were other ways to see his work. Dore Ashton looked at DIVER and complained, "What about these objects [attached to the canvas]? It is impossible in this painting to decide just what merit they have."[95] And in 1964, Sidney Tillim said, "It seems ridiculous to speak of the *decline* of an artist not yet thirty-five years old. Yet such is the conclusion I feel one has to draw from the Jasper Johns retrospective at the Jewish Museum. . . . He has . . . been unable to achieve a really major style. . . . Where Johns is really vulnerable is in his dependence on ideas which are exhausted rapidly."[96]

The characteristic progression of Johns' work is perhaps easier to see now than it was a decade ago. There is a recurrent feature of his paintings—a sense of impasses created, explored, and finally overcome, with a subsequent burst of new freedom. The results of his new freedom are clearly seen in two very different paintings which follow ACCORDING TO WHAT.

EDDINGSVILLE. 1965. See Plate 120

EDDINGSVILLE (1965) incorporates many of the images of its predecessor, but in a much freer, more spontaneous way. It has a less logical quality, and it conveys a more pleasurable sensation. It exists, as if to say that the same elements can be used another way, but there is also a different feeling.

Another painting, FLAGS (1965), appeared in *Time* magazine: "With the advent of op art, somebody was sure to paint something not really there. And now Jasper Johns has done it, by painting a U.S. flag . . . that appears only in the eye's retina. High school students of science know the trick: colors produce afterimages of their complements."[97]

STUDIO. 1964. See Plate 119

Johns described knowing about this optical feature of perception, and the fact that he finally used it, in this way: "People know well that if you drop a glass on the floor, it will break. But some go through life never dropping glasses. For me, this painting was like dropping a glass."

The idea of the imprint—the trace of something pressed literally into the paint surface—had meanwhile been further elaborated. We can trace this from the DEVICE CIRCLE of 1959, through NO (1961), in which a bronze cast of Duchamp's *Feuille de Vigne Femelle (Female Fig Leaf)* was pressed into the encaustic surface ("it was something metal that could be heated and pressed into the wax, and it was something I had around the studio"), through the artist's own handprints, footprints, armprints, until finally we have STUDIO and STUDIO 2, in 1964 and 1966,[98] where the screen door, a palmetto leaf, and windows of the studio leave their literal imprint. The trace of natural and architectural elements leads directly to the origin of a new image, and a major painting, HARLEM LIGHT (1967).

It has a peculiar background. Johns was taking a taxi to the airport,

STUDIO 2. 1966. See Plate 128

traveling through Harlem, when he passed a small store which had a wall painted to resemble flagstones. He decided it would appear in his next painting. Some weeks later when he began the painting, he asked David Whitney to find the flagstone wall, and photograph it. Whitney returned to say he could not find the wall anywhere. Johns himself then looked for the wall, driving back and forth across Harlem, searching for what he had briefly seen. He never found it, and finally had to conclude that it had been painted over or demolished. Thus he was obliged to re-create the flagstone wall from memory. This distressed him. "What I had hoped to do was an exact copy of the wall. It was red, black, and gray, but I'm sure that it didn't look like what I did. But I did my best."

HARLEM LIGHT. 1967. See Plate 129

Explaining further, he said: "Whatever I do seems artificial and false, to me. They—whoever painted the wall—had an idea; I doubt that whatever they did had to conform to anything except their own pleasure. I wanted to use that design. The trouble is that when you start to work, you can't eliminate your own sophistication. If I could have traced it I would have felt secure that I had it right. Because what's interesting to me is the fact that it isn't designed, but taken. It's not mine."

This is an extremely difficult stance to comprehend. What does it matter that he couldn't get it exactly? Isn't it the artist's job to make things up for others to enjoy? Probably we are facing here two aspects of Johns' working attitudes. The first is his desire to "work on other levels"; he does not want to invent the flagstone design, but to transform it once given. That transformation is obscured in a sense, if nothing is given in the first instance. The second idea has to do with "small differences"; one suspects he feels acutely that he cannot re-create the nuances of the original; in working from scratch, he smooths out the roughness, simplifying what is not really so simple—in short, imposing his own sophistication.

Does it matter? Objectively, Johns' flagstones may or may not be noticeably different from the original;[99] but he is probably correct in suspecting that his flagstones are not the same as the flagstones some naive painter made, and he is probably right that the picture would have had a different impact had he worked from a photograph, or a tracing, of the original.

Nevertheless he didn't, and the flagstone section of HARLEM LIGHT, once done, was immediately taken as an impersonal image, to be used in further work. Before going on, however, it is worth noticing that this superb painting exemplifies another Johns dictum, as found in his notebooks: ". . . to see that something has happened. Is this best shown by 'pointing' to it or by 'hiding' it?" In HARLEM LIGHT a painted-out black swatch crosses two canvas panels. It is hidden, but so visible that it immediately draws the eye. Johns observes: "That's what hiding is—you know it still exists."

The flagstones, we might note in passing, are an ideal Johnsian image, although a surprising one. Like the early flags, they are man-made; they have a referent in reality; they have a pattern that can be seen as abstract or concrete; they have fixed proportions that limit the area of artistic invention; and they were, originally, taken from the artist's experience, not from his imagination.

55

VOICE. 1964–67. Oil on canvas with objects, 243.8 x 176.6 cm (8' x 5'9½"). Private collection

VOICE. 1966–67. Lithograph. 122.5 x 80.6 cm (48¼ x 31¾"). Published by ULAE.

SCREEN PIECE. 1967. See Plate 131

The flagstones appear again and again in later work. So does another image of 1967, first seen in the literally titled SCREEN PIECE: the fork and spoon with the directions, FORK SHOULD BE 7" LONG. The presence of eating utensils reminds us of Johns' comment that "my work feeds upon itself"; in this case, it literally does.

Johns made a two-paneled painting VOICE (1964–67) which included a wire with a spoon and fork. He later made a print of VOICE, in which he incorporated the wire, spoon, and fork. These elements were photographed from the original painting to make a photographic plate for the print. Instructing the printers, Johns wrote on the photograph "Fork should be 7" long," the dimension in the final VOICE print.

Later he found the photo lying around the studio. By then it seemed like an object to him, a thing available for use. He was struck by the small photo with his written instruction to make the image life-size; he decided to enlarge the image to much greater than life-size, but to leave the original instruction. He silkscreened the image onto canvases, and then painted over them. SCREEN PIECE may be a perplexing final result, but evidently it suggests a past, and an origin, even a mundane origin—which in fact it has.

SCREEN PIECE reminds us of a curious inversion in Johns' own work. When he first began lithography, he used images derived from his paintings. With time, he modified the print images with increasing subtlety, until they departed more and more from the paintings. But it was almost impossible that his experience in lithography should not eventually provide a subject matter for painting, and SCREEN PIECE and SCREEN PIECE 2 (1968) are the first concrete evidence of this. Eventually, of course, he did DECOY, a painting that followed the print of the same name. If nothing else, this suggests that Johns' work as an artist obliges us to recognize that his printing is not a sideline to painting, but rather is as important as the painting itself. SCREEN PIECE is mysterious, but it is utterly unfathomable without the understanding of his interest in printmaking, and the interaction of his experiences in printing and painting.

The title is often a clue, in this regard. Whenever Johns begins a new area, his titles are literal in a way that later elaborations are not. SCREEN PIECE is literal the way FLAG (1955) or the PAINTED BRONZES (1960) are literal; it is Sufi-literal, implacably literal.

Mention must be made of Johns' enormous painting, MAP, for Expo '67 in Montreal. It is a huge painting, over 15 by 30 feet, based on Buckminster Fuller's dymaxion conception of spatial topography. One ought to emphasize the size of this work. ACCORDING TO WHAT is a huge painting; but the dymaxion MAP is nearly four times as large. Not only that, but the panels were painted a second time—after Johns saw it in place, and became dissatisfied with what he had done. (In passing, we might note that this enormous effort to repaint, to retrieve a false start, is characteristic of his methods. Some artists let it go, saying that their work represents their feelings at the time; Johns reconsiders, even at great cost to himself.) Of MAP, Lawrence Alloway said: "In appearance the painting is ungainly, splayed jaggedly on the wall, taking its form from Fuller's triangulation.

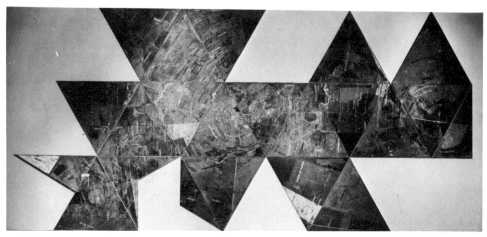

MAP (based on Buckminster Fuller's Dymaxion Airocean World). 1967–71. Encaustic and collage on canvas, 4.72 x 10.06 m (15′6″ x 33′). Museum Ludwig, Cologne

This is not, I think, a failure on Johns's part; on the contrary, it is a part of his move away from the elegant paradoxes of his early work to a brute style, of which this unruly painting is a climax."[100]

This has subsequently proved correct.

In his painting, the late 1960s seem to have been a period of difficulty, of reworking, of labored effort. On the other hand, his prints show a renewed exuberance, exemplified by the brilliant series of FIGURES IN COLOR done at Gemini in 1969 (see plate 139). Their history is interesting.

In 1968, he went to California and did a series of ten numerals in black-and-white. Each was printed from one lithograph stone and one aluminum plate. Unlike ordinary lithographic procedure, in which the stones are effaced after the edition is run off, these were retained, and a year later, he did a colored series from the same stones.[101] The colors were applied laterally—in a sketchbook note, Johns originally considered applying them vertically—with a roller inked with a spectrum of colors.

A good insight into Johns' method of working comes from examination of the progression of colors. Johns had no thought except to begin at zero with the primary colors—red, blue, yellow—and to finish at nine with the secondary colors—orange, green, purple. In between he was obliged to have a series of transformations. These can be explained as a succession of additions and subtractions. That is, FIGURE 0 is blue-yellow-red. FIGURE 1 is yellow and red, add blue giving purple, the new top band. FIGURE 2 is red and purple, subtract red, giving blue, the top band. FIGURE 3 is purple and blue, add yellow; and so forth. A similar progression was used in Johns' 1963 0–9 lithographs, and like those lithographs, there is a discontinuity—at some point in the progression, you must have an illogical step in order to come out with the correct final result.

No one will notice this, of course. The color numerals have an exquisite life of their own, and whether the color bands are arbitrarily or logically applied is a fine point, of interest more for what it tells us about Johns than what it tells us about the impact of the work itself.

But if this lithograph work is wholeheartedly beautiful, his paintings at this time were difficult. Not only the dymaxion MAP, but the three panels of VOICE 2 (1971) were painted more than once.

VOICE 2 can be related to an earlier painting, FOOL'S HOUSE (1962). In FOOL'S HOUSE the title is split to suggest a curved space—that is, if the canvas which we see flat on the wall were actually curved in a cylinder, then the title letters would read continuously as one walked counterclockwise around the canvas. Johns did not actually make this space; he merely provides clues to suggest another space. Similarly a flat map contains clues that it represents a curved reality, the globe of the earth.

It is likely that Johns' work on the dymaxion MAP reawakened these thoughts of curvature. VOICE 2 is also intended to represent a curved space; that is why the panels can be arranged in several different orders. In Johns' notebook directions, they can be hung as

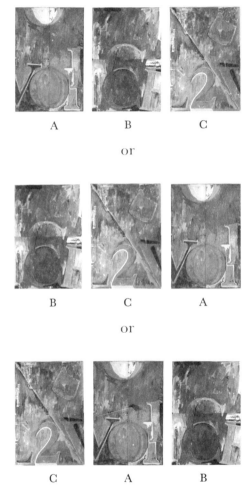

This is the equivalent of having the three canvases bent into a circle, which seen from above looks like this:

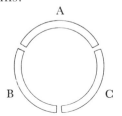

In other words, a walk around this imagined circle would give various possibilities for the order of the canvases, depending on where one started. The fact that they are presented as flat—with the circular space only suggested—leads to questions of "matching," of congruity, which has been a significant idea in all his work since 1971.

For example, there is DECOY (1971), a lithograph without an antecedent painting. DECOY—so named because "it was supposed to draw the birds"—stands in a similar position to his prints as ACCORDING TO WHAT does to his paintings seven years before. It is a catalog of Johnsian imagery, a summary of many years of work.[102] Taken purely as a print, it incorporates elements of the prints PASSAGE I and PASSAGE II—notably the bent spectrum and the cast leg; the ALE CANS; and below, in boxes, the panoply of flag, flashlight, light bulb, ale cans, paintbrushes, and numbers. Overall the composition suggests an inverted "target with plaster casts," but it is distinctly a print, and not a painting.

DECOY. 1971. Lithograph, 104.1 x 73.7 cm (41 x 29″). Published by ULAE

In fact, one can think of DECOY as PASSAGE III. Years before, Johns made his two PASSAGE prints, and then attempted a third version, which was to consist of elements from the earlier prints, rotated about an axis. He abandoned the project when he found that the rotation was unclear; the idea behind the print could not be discerned by the observer. But he revived this idea with DECOY, in presenting elements of former work in a new perspective, a new spatial orientation. For anyone who knows Johns' work, the impulse to "match up" this image with others he has already done is almost overpowering; the title suggests that this effort is false—the work is a decoy, deluding the follower—but the impulse to assemble fragments and ideas remains.

Another example of "matching," and of an imagined space hinted at—but not represented—by the configuration of the paintings, is shown in UNTITLED (1972). This is a four-panel painting. On the right, there is a panel of wood strips, to which wax casts of body parts are attached. The two middle panels are flagstone sections. The left-hand panel is an image of "cross-hatching," a new Johnsian image, later to be elaborated in its own right.

UNTITLED. 1972. See Plate 148

Like the flagstones, the cross-hatching idea derived from a fleeting visual experience. "I was riding in a car, going out to the Hamptons for the weekend, when a car came in the opposite direction. It was covered with these marks, but I only saw it for a moment—then it was gone—just a brief glimpse. But I immediately thought that I would use it for my next painting."

The experience, and the image, remind us of the flagstones—man-made marks, glimpsed from a passing car, making an indelible impression. But the appearance of cross-hatching in UNTITLED (1972) must be examined more closely. And we must also ask about another new element, the casts and wooden strips of the right-hand panel.

Originally, Johns had the idea of cutting holes in the canvas, and pasting the casts onto the canvas flaps. But the flaps would have fallen down under the weight of the casts. And the panel would be unwieldy for movement and storage. So he settled on wooden strips, fastened by wing nuts. Having decided that, he felt that he ought to number them, and color-code them, for easy assembly and disassembly (dismemberment). But anyone looking at UNTITLED must start by wondering what these four panels are doing together in the first place. A kind of visual coherence is provided by the similar size of the elements: the cross-hatching, the flagstones, the cast pieces. Some unity is implied. Further, we notice a progressive abstraction, from the concrete reality of the casts, through the representation of the flagstones, to the final figurative abstraction of the cross-hatching in secondary colors. We go from things to marks—or more obscurely, from specific casts of things to marks which may stand for any number of things (and which in architectural drawings usually stand for a blank surface. From the specific to the unspecific, from three-dimensionality to flatness.[103]

At the same time, we are left with some open questions. Indeed, the painting seems to imply an arbitrary self-limitation. The panels are so discontinuous, that we might suspect more panels at either end.

This is a feature of Johns' work: the interplay between pictures that are closed and self-contained, like the flags, and pictures that are open and expansive. The self-contained pictures have always been easier to deal with than the open ones—and UNTITLED is distinctively open.

Its secrets seem to lie in the juxtaposition of the four panels. Looking at the midpoint between the two flagstone panels, one notices that while the two panels have the same "subject matter," the break between them is peculiar, and disturbing. It bothers the eye. The junction doesn't make sense in a picture that implies a hidden sense of order. Why are the two flagstone panels divided in that way?

There is an answer, and a perfectly logical one. The panels overlap. If, in your mind, you move the right-hand flagstone panel midway over the left-hand panel, you get a congruity—a matching—that actually implies a secret square in the middle of it all; there we have an "imaginary unit," a painting within the painting.

The cross-hatching panel of UNTITLED (1972) has since become the principal motif, the chief visual language of his most recent work. The paintings from 1973–76 are all cross-hatching paintings.

CORPSE AND MIRROR (1974) is a largely black-and-white painting in two panels which immediately suggests a further extension of Johns' concerns with matching. The right-hand side is a mirror of the left; so much for the mirror. Why the corpse? Johns is mute on this point, but it clearly belongs to art history. The Surrealists, according to André Breton, devised a game— actually a child's game—using a piece of paper folded into several sections:

EXQUISITE CORPSE.–*Game of folded paper which consists in having several people compose a phrase or a drawing collectively, none of the participants having any idea of the nature of the preceding contribution or contributions. The now classical*

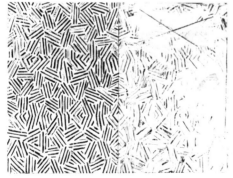

CORPSE AND MIRROR. 1974. See Plate 162

example, which gave its name to the game, is the first phrase obtained in this manner: The exquisite—corpse—shall drink—the young—wine.[104]

Johns has said that he did this work by painting the sections of the left-hand panel without reference of one to another. He then created a modified mirror image of his work on the right-hand panel. Thus the corpse, and thus the mirror of the corpse.[105]

This idea of the corpse and mirror, of the panels related to each other in various ways, suggested a number of ideas—as the original flags had triggered ideas. And we might note in passing that just as the paintings of 1955–58 seemed to emerge fully elaborated, a coherent and self-contained body of work, so too do his cross-hatching paintings of 1974–76 stand as a complete body of ideas in a new visual idiom.

In this case, the ideas concern the cross-hatched lines and the way they intersect various panels of the paintings. The ideas are directed to two ends. One is the notion of visual search—in SCENT, for example—and the other is the idea of the stand-in, the surrogate, in THE DUTCH WIVES. (A Dutch wife is a board with a hole, used by sailors as a surrogate for a woman.) Thus Johns continues his concerns with the painting-as-object, a thing in itself; with the painting as a subject for searching inquiry, a target; and with the painting as a stand-in for some reality, a substitute, an artificial creation which "represents" something else.

The working methods which led to their creation varies. THE BARBER'S TREE (1975), painted in flesh-and-blood colors, and suggestive of a striped barber pole, was actually provoked by a photograph in the *National Geographic*.[106] (The picture showed a Mexican barber who had painted his tree.) It was probably the underlying idea of painting over reality that interested Johns.

THE DUTCH WIVES (1975), two panels in subtle blacks and grays, are a kind of reverie on duplication. They are done in encaustic, and the newspaper strips are repeated in the two panels. One thinks of Rauschenberg's *Factum I* and *Factum II* as antecedents of this duplication, but those paintings were a response to the supposed spontaneity of Abstract Expressionism. Johns' concerns are distinctly different, and relate more to his mirror images and his doubles; to his idea that having done something once, it could be done again differently. The painting seems to ask what the difference is, or what constitutes a difference in the mind's eye. In this regard it is interesting that the two panels of THE DUTCH WIVES are not identical, as some observers have seen them to be. Their edges are largely identical, but as one moves toward the indistinct center, the difference between the panels becomes more pronounced.

The fascination with distinctions at the borders is continued with UN-TITLED (1975), a painting which explores a geometrical idea; to provide all the possibilities for interactions in a single painting. UNTITLED is a square image composed of four panels, one large and three small rectangles. The large panel is arranged in such a way that the top and bottom, and right and left edges are the same—that is, if red lines run off at the top, they will run off at the same position on the bottom, and so on.

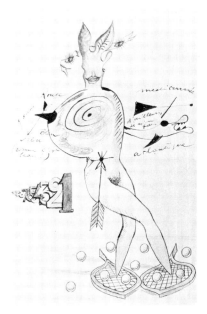

Yves Tanguy, Joan Miró, Max Morise, and Man Ray. *Figure (Cadavre exquis).* 1926–27. The Museum of Modern Art, New York

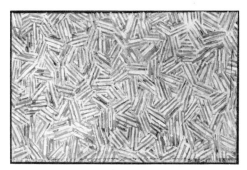

THE BARBER'S TREE. 1975. See Plate 166

The Barber's Tree. Photograph by Charles O'Rear

61

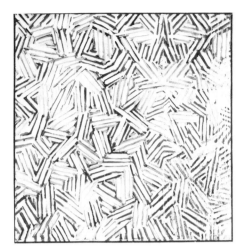

UNTITLED. 1975. Oil, encaustic, and collage on canvas, 127.3 x 127.3 cm (50⅛ x 50⅛″). Private collection

SCENT. 1973–74. See Plate 161

As for the adjacent smaller panels, there are five junctions. Reading down, they are ordered in this way: 1) the lines are mirror images; 2) directions of line and colors change; 3) colors continue but directions change; 4) directions continue but colors change; 5) directions and colors continue unchanged.

If the organization of this painting is fairly simple, the underlying structure of SCENT (1973–74) is more intricate, and more tantalizing. This is a large painting in three panels. Its title suggests the hunt; it also recalls Jackson Pollock's last painting, of the same name. At first it appears to be only a random array of secondary colors, green, orange, and purple painted with a distinctness that evokes the flagstones. Then one notices that it is not really random, since no cross-hatched area abuts another area of the same color. A second order is suggested by the faintly visible vertical lines that divide each panel into three sections. (That Johns did not obscure these lines reminds us of his ideas about "hiding".[107]) Thus it can be considered a painting with nine vertical elements. From FOOL'S HOUSE and VOICE 2, we are alerted to the idea of a curved space, as indicated by a congruity of the extreme right- and left-hand borders of the painting. We find it again in SCENT: the first element on the extreme left of the painting is the same as the ninth element on the extreme right. Continuing with this idea, we see that the elements which abut the junctions between canvases are always identical. Only the middle element of each canvas is unique. In other words, if the three vertical elements of the first canvas were labeled A B C, the second canvas would be C D E, and the third E F A. The possibility that the canvases could be rearranged is clearly indicated.

The cross-hatching motif first appeared in association with flagstones, and in his recent painting, END PAPER (1976), Johns returns to the association. It is a dark, rather grim painting in secondary colors, different from the liveliness of CORPSE AND MIRROR II, or UNTITLED (1975). END PAPER is notable for the visual equation of the two motifs; here Johns has straightened the edges of the flagstones to make them reiterate the composition of the cross-hatching. By doing so Johns emphasizes both motifs as units within a superimposed structure, as the earlier alphabets were units within a structure. This association with alphabets is fitting, for the title derives from Johns' collaboration on a book with Samuel Beckett.[108] The book was published in 1976, and these two images, the flagstones and the cross-hatching, form the endpapers.

For the moment Johns has settled into a series of paintings which elaborate on patterns of cross-hatching. He has already begun to complicate these patterns in difficult ways; one senses that eventually he will have exhausted the potential for the mathematical manipulation of the image, or that his complexities will have passed beyond the ability of anyone else to see what he has done. That will no doubt provoke another crisis in his career, another endpoint from which he must begin anew. For an artist who has already survived so many crises so brilliantly, we can be sure he will arrive at another motif, another set of concerns, another way of expressing his ideas. He will work himself into a bind, and then he will break free, and move onward, as he has always done, to our benefit and pleasure.

In summary, what can we say of his methods of working? The question is not idle, for if a Johns painting does not reveal his emotions, it certainly reveals his intellectual attitudes, and something that might be called his philosophy of life.

"Right conduct," John Cage called it.[109] Some years later Barbara Rose elaborated:

> [Johns is] perhaps the only artist operating today in the dimension of a mental physics, that is of a true metaphysic. We infer that Johns sees no separation between decisions made in art and those made in life. His decisions have unmistakable moral implications, for he is among those artists for whom the activity on the canvas is the exemplar of his understanding of right human conduct.[110]

What of that conduct? A strong sense of acceptance of things as they are—surely an undercurrent in his willingness to use pre-existing imagery and objects. The belief that something, once begun, must be carried to a conclusion—an attitude that shows in his attempts to retrieve a painting, to rework it, even at the expense of an elegance and finesse which usually characterize his work. The doubtful interplay between what you see and what you know, what you see and what you observe, which is both anxiety-provoking and fascinating at the same time.

Beyond this, we may look for some idea of the artist himself, as he portrays his own role in his work. Since Johns works with alternatives, mirror images, and oppositions, it is not surprising that we can form two opposite ideas about him. In one sense he, like the late Adlai Stevenson, is a man so extraordinarily intelligent, so deeply aware of his choices, that he perpetually risks frozen indecision. He is able to proceed only by the most stiffly arbitrary maneuvers—to use what is already there, to accept what is given, to proceed on the basis of what has already happened. It is this aspect which has led some to view Johns as a limited, inhibited artist, entangled in his own past, forever forced to confront logical impasses which are, in the end, entirely of his own making.

But in the mirror image he is Harry Houdini, the magician who patiently shows you his constraints—the handcuffs and ropes and the locked trunk—and yet escapes from his self-imposed bonds in the nick of time. Watching him, we are fairly sure he knows a way out; even so we wonder whether he will make a mistake, a fatal slip. Houdini creates illusions, but they are still dangerous illusions.

The artist as thinker and the artist as magician are conceptions as old as Daedalus and Merlin, but in the twentieth century they have taken on new meanings. Modern history provides fresh urgency to the most ancient of mythological warnings—that man must live with the consequences of his creations. Johns always does precisely this. And when he says, "The problem is not doing something, the problem is knowing what one wants to do," we recognize a peculiarly modern dilemma.

As for his own attitude toward working, here are two recent notebook entries:

I have meant what I have done. OR—I have often meant what I have done. OR—I have sometimes meant what I have done. OR—I have tried to mean what I was doing.

And again:

To Give Up
Or
To Do the Work
To Doubt that the Work Needs Doing?
At any rate, the time passes.

NOTES

1. There is disagreement about whether artistic activity springs from conflict. In the psychoanalytic literature it comes down to what you call conflict, and what you call artistic activity. Certainly the view that artistic activity is the product of sickness—art as manifest neurosis—is no longer tenable. The late Lawrence Kubie wrote: "Unconscious conflicts and necessities which are carried over from the nursery, from childhood, and from schooling, reappear in many disguised forms throughout life. They may be expressed in an effort to disprove something which is true; or conversely they may drive a man to attempt to prove the impossible. Or they may drive the creative zeal blindly in an effort to resolve some ancient dilemma, to pay an old debt or settle an old grudge, to achieve the unattainable goal of a childhood fantasy, or to lift the curse from something which in childhood had been an overwhelming source of pain, humiliation, and terror." This is the traditional view which Kubie himself was influential in discarding. But in a person's life there are plenty of conflicts which are healthy, and particularly when one recognizes that all art forms thrive on the expression of some inner conflict—whether we call it counterpoint, composition, or drama—one cannot shake off the suspicion that, in the end, the activity reflects a conflict within the artist himself (Lawrence S. Kubie, *Neurotic Distortion of the Creative Process,* Noonday, New York, 1970, pp. 60–61).

2. Some, like Andy Warhol, have even made mechanical reproduction central in their work. "The reason I'm painting this way is that I want to be a machine, and I feel that whatever I do and do machine-like is what I want to do." (G.R. Swenson, "What is Pop Art? Part I," *Art News,* 62, Nov. 1963, p. 26.)

3. "While you are alone you are entirely your own master and if you have one companion you are but half your own, and the less so in proportion to the indiscretion of his behavior. And if you have many companions you will fall deeper into the same trouble. . . . I tell you, you will not be able to help often listening to their chatter." (*Treatise on Painting,* in *The Notebooks of Leonardo da Vinci,* ed. Jean Paul Richter, Peter Smith, New York, 1970, vol. 1, p. 248.)

4. Johns: "I was working in a bookstore, and you had little rectangular pads of paper to write orders on. I used to fold these sheets and then tear them, so that when they were opened the tears made a symmetrical design. This collage was a collection of torn sheets. The idea was to make something symmetrical that didn't appear to be symmetrical."

5. Johns: "I was interested in the idea of a painting that did more than one thing, that had another aspect. That was the reason for the sound."

6. The face is that of Rachel Rosenthal (now Moody); she is the owner of the piece.

7. STAR was his first commission. He had done a painting in the shape of a cross, and Rachel Rosenthal said she would buy it if it were a Jewish star. Johns made one; she bought it.

8. Max Kozloff, *Jasper Johns,* Abrams, New York, 1969, p. 15.

9. Edgar Allan Poe, "The Philosophy of Composition" (1846), in *The Selected Poetry and Prose,* Modern Library, New York, 1951, p. 370.

10. Leo Steinberg, "Jasper Johns: The First Seven Years of His Art" (1962), *Other Criteria: Confrontations with Twentieth-Century Art,* Oxford University Press, New York, 1972, p. 31.

11. Johns, quoted in Walter Hopps, "An Interview with Jasper Johns," *Artforum,* 3, March 1965, p. 34.

12. William S. Baring-Gould, ed., *The Annotated Sherlock Holmes* [by Sir Arthur Conan Doyle], Clarkson N. Potter, New York, 1967, vol. I, p. 349.

13. Johns has done monochromatic targets, beginning with GREEN TARGET (1955), but such treatment of the symbol merely emphasizes the nature of targets by eliminating contrasting colors. In addition, there is a tendency in Johns to explore the attributes of a thing through deprivation. One way to know that our ordinary conception of a target involves contrasting colors is to see it without such contrast. (Leo Castelli did not see the target in GREEN TARGET when he first saw the painting.)

14. "His Heart Belongs to Dada," *Time,* 73, May 4, 1959, p. 58.

15. Kozloff, *op. cit.,* p. 21. Kozloff is actually referring to TENNYSON (1958).

16. A note of caution: Often John's "laborious efforts" to cover actually draw attention to what has happened. One may speculate that the layered meanings in a Johns work have their analogue in the layers of paint and wax that sometimes conceal, sometimes reveal, what lies beneath. That is one way to look at it. Another way is to recognize that he is a painter whose interest in process leads him to reveal the process—as an action over time—to the viewer. That is, a series of events and decisions led to the final picture; Johns often seems as interested in the sequence of steps as he is in the final result—at least, he often tries to show "what happened" along the way. It may be exaggerated to say that a Johns painting contains its own biography, but that kind of idea is present in many pictures.

Occasionally his working methods cause curatorial problems. One long-standing question concerns the date of his first FLAG painting, originally purchased by Philip Johnson in 1958, and now in the collection of the Museum of Modern Art. The painting was dated 1954, but Johns argued that it was done in 1955. Recently someone noticed that the collage included newsprint from 1956, and the museum wanted to change the date accordingly. Johns stated that the picture was damaged in his studio in 1956, and that he repaired it that year, but that the painting was still properly dated 1955. He also points out that certain early works include collage elements that are old—much older than the paintings themselves—thus obviating entirely such direct methods of dating.

17. The painter and critic Sidney Tillim observed, "Johns' paintings and drawings of numbers . . . are drawn as if they should have been apples." ("Ten Years of Jasper Johns," *Arts Magazine,* 38, April 1964, p. 22.) The review was unsympathetic; perhaps Tillim wanted to contradict the comment of Edward Lucie-Smith that "Johns' innovations, especially his use of signs and letters buried in the paint, have continued to bear fruit. . . ." ("Round the New York Art Galleries: Letters and Figures," *The Listener,* Jan. 10, 1963, p. 71.)

18. *Time, loc. cit.* About this comment Johns later said, "I mean that one shouldn't approach a work of art with a preexisting attitude. . . . (laughing) But then someone pointed out to me that I had gone and boxed-in all my radiators, so you didn't see them!"

19. Kozloff, *op. cit.,* p. 16.

20. Emily Genauer *(New York Herald Tribune,* 119, April 3, 1960, section 4, p. 7) noted that Johns "likes to attach empty coke bottles to his canvas," a reference to Rauschenberg's *Curfew* (1958). Apparently she never discovered the difference. In the *Sunday Herald Tribune Magazine,* 124, Sept. 6, 1964, p. 21, she spoke of "Johns' oversized abstractions complete with appended coke bottles and dirty brooms."

21. Calvin Tomkins, *The Bride and the Bachelors,* Viking, New York, 1965. p. 213 (hereafter: Tomkins, *The Bride and the Bachelors).*

22. Johns has been artistic director for the Cunningham company since 1967. The set based on *The Large Glass* was first seen in Buffalo, N.Y., March 10, 1968.

23. June 20, 1961. David Tudor played *Variation II* by John Cage at the American Embassy theater in Paris. The participating artists were Robert Rauschenberg, Niki de Saint-Phalle, Jean Tinguely, and Jasper Johns. Along with the target, Johns made ENTR'ACTE, which was brought onstage during the intermission.

24. The year before he had painted the racing FALSE START and the somber, contradictory JUBILEE. The attachment of emotional values to his work is never easy, but there is often a kind of pairing—seen most recently in the creamy warmth of THE BARBER'S TREE (1975), and the well-titled WEEPING WOMEN (1975).

25. Rauschenberg was, and still is, an extraordinarily forceful personality. Everyone who works with him or around him recognizes it. Tatyana Grosman, in the early days of ULAE, recalls "I really wanted to invite Rauschenberg [before Johns] but I was a little afraid that I might not be strong enough, that he would be too disruptive": Calvin Tomkins, "Profile: Tatyana Grosman," *The New Yorker,* 52, June 7, 1976, p. 62 (hereafter: Tomkins, "Profile: Tatyana Grosman"). Ken Tyler, when he was master printer at Gemini G.E.L., said, "Everything goes crazy when Rauschenberg is here. You work his hours, his way, nonstop around the clock. It's incredibly exciting and incredibly exhausting. When he finally leaves you sleep for two days straight. But there's no denying Bob."

From this standpoint, Castelli observes that "even though Jasper was around Bob all the time, he was entirely original right from the start. It is really quite remarkable that anyone could stand up to Bob's personality in that way. It shows the strength of Jasper's own personality."

26. Johns relates the idea of painting the sides of the canvas to his earlier notion of provoking the spectator to move around the picture, and to see it from many sides.

27. Barbara Rose, "The Graphic Work of Jasper Johns: Part II," *Artforum,* 8, Sept. 1970, p. 71 (hereafter: Rose, "Graphic Work of Jasper Johns, II"). There are no flagstones in any of the five SCREEN PIECE paintings. The author was probably thinking of WALL PIECE (1968) or HARLEM LIGHT (1967).

28. Hopps, *op. cit.,* p. 35.

29. A particularly severe example of a self-imposed limitation is Alfred Hitchcock's film *Rope* (1948). The picture was shot in a succession of single takes, without cuts. Why would Hitchcock burden himself with the most exasperating technical difficulties, in order simultaneously to deprive himself of the ability to cut, which is the most powerful and unique tool of film? It is a decision so aberrant as to seem almost self-destructive, yet there is an excitement in the challenge of overcoming limitations.

30. The situation is actually more complicated than this. A non-choice is itself a choice; that is, to select ready-made elements represents a decision *not* to make them, and this has meaning. On one level it implies something about the artist's use of his own time and skills, since he could always make the object if he wanted to. Consider FLASHLIGHT III (1958), where the raw materials to make the flashlight merge with the partially created thing. Kozloff sees the flashlight as sinking into its base, but it is just as easy to view it as emerging from its origins, or even as being unearthed, like an archaeological artifact. In any case it reminds us of the peculiar power of an unfinished work of art to draw

attention to the artist's skills. (Michelangelo's unfinished *Slaves* seem to tell us more about the sculptor's talent than the polished, complete *David.*)

But there is another level of complexity to ready-made objects. Although it suggests a non-choice, there is inevitably a selection among various alternatives. Johns wanted an "ordinary" flashlight for his first sculpture. But when he went out to buy one he couldn't find the kind he had in mind. He was obliged to look very hard for the commonplace object—it wasn't commonplace at all. This is obviously no "found object."

31. FLAG ON ORANGE FIELD and the small WHITE FLAG were in Bonwit Teller's windows in 1957–58. Such exposure for his work must have emphasized to Johns the object-ness of his pictures.

32. *Artists of the New York School: Second Generation,* The Jewish Museum, New York, 1957. As a curious historical incident, a Johns painting was seen at the Stable Gallery in 1956, as part of a Rauschenberg painting. In those days, artists of the Stable Gallery could each propose two new painters to be included in an annual show at the gallery. Rauschenberg intended to propose his ex-wife, Susan Weil, and Johns. But that year the gallery changed its policy, so Rauschenberg made a canvas with two doors, and behind the doors he put a small Johns flag and a small Weil painting; this painting was subsequently exhibited.

Leo Castelli later acquired the Rauschenberg with the two doors. He kept the painting in his warehouse. One day he examined the painting and discovered that the Johns flag had been stolen. Castelli recalls a final incident in the story:

Years later, a dealer—we do not need to say who—came to me and said, "Someone has brought me this Johns painting and I don't know it, and I wondered if you could tell me about it, the date and so on." I knew immediately what it was; it was the stolen painting. I said, "The painting has been stolen and I would like to keep it right here. I don't want it to leave my gallery." But this person said he had promised the person he got it from, and he didn't feel he could leave it with me, and he said he would have to talk to the other person, and he was very insistent. So I said, "Well, all right." I never saw the painting again.

33. He had previously had a gallery in Paris, before World War II; he described himself as a playboy, in *Holiday* (M. Elkoff, "Antic Arts: Leo Castelli: the Artful Entrepreneur"), 37, June 1965, p. 99.

34. Because his name is so unusual, a number of people have suspected that Jasper Johns made it up himself. (He didn't; his name is Jasper Johns, Jr.) The origin of the name is suggested by Charles F. Stuckey ("Johns:

Yet waving?" *Art in America,* 64, May–June 1976, p. 5):

Perhaps only a curious coincidence related to Johns' flags is the existence of several 19th-century works of art that portray the heroism of one Sergeant William Jasper: the two best known are Emanuel Leutze's *Sergeant Jasper Rescuing the Flag on Fort Moultrie,* 1859, and Alexander Doyle's 1888 bronze in Madison Square, Savannah. Jasper, one of the South's most glorious Revolutionary heroes, distinguished himself by twice recovering our fallen flag (during the bombardment of Charleston Harbor, June 1776, and in the assault upon Savannah, Oct. 1779). Was Jasper Johns in some way the namesake of the famous soldier? I wonder whether the school books in South Carolina, where he spent his childhood, underlined for Johns the brave daring of the hero who kept our flag visible.

As a boy Johns was shown a statue of Sergeant Jasper by his father, who told him that the figure was the namesake of them both.

35. Barbara Rose, "Decoys and Doubles: Jasper Johns and the Modernist Mind," *Arts Magazine,* 50, May 1976, p. 69 (hereafter: Rose, "Decoys and Doubles").

36. Tomkins, *The Bride and the Bachelors,* p. 213.

37. Barbara Rose, *American Art Since 1900,* rev. ed., Praeger, New York, 1975, p. 179 (hereafter: Rose, *American Art Since 1900*).

38. *Ibid.,* p. 210.

39. "In the Galleries," *Arts,* 32, Jan. 1958, p. 55.

40. *Time, loc. cit.*

41. Leo Steinberg, "Contemporary Art and the Plight of Its Public" (1962), *Other Criteria: Confrontations with Twentieth-Century Art,* Oxford University Press, New York, 1972, p.13.

42. In fact, art is just as likely as any other area of human endeavor to form an Establishment which becomes fixed and finally ossified. (So is physics. Max Planck once said that physics does not advance by the dispassionate weighing of new ideas, but rather by having the old men with the wrong ideas die off.)

43. Certainly Alfred Barr saw it that way. In a letter to Johns, dated 27 August 1959, he wrote:

I am sending you an advance copy of our new Bulletin on paintings and sculptures added to our collection during 1958. A friend . . . asked me whether there was any special significance in my having reproduced your three pictures in one cut instead of individually. I . . . intended to emphasize the fact that we had acquired three. . . . As you know, the Museum and I myself have been under some criticism for having bought three works by one artist and he rather little known. I think the Bulletin emphasizes rather than soft pedals this controversial action.

44. Ben Heller, "Jasper Johns," *School of New York: Some Younger Artists,* ed. B. H. Friedman, Grove Press, New York, 1959, p. 30.

45. "If the end of an art style may be marked by the moment when no young painters of the first rank choose to work within it, then 1960 constitutes such a date for Abstract Expressionism." (Rose, *American Art Since 1900,* pp. 179–80.)

46. Apparently he was not so coolheaded at the time. Mrs. Catherine Rembert, one of Johns' teachers at the University of South Carolina, was to have dinner with him on the night of his first one-man show. Johns arrived late, "picked her up and danced her about the room. The Museum of Modern Art had just bought three of his paintings for its permanent collection." In D. R. Dickborn, "Art's Fair-Haired Boy," *The State* (Columbia, S.C.), Jan. 15, 1961, pp.20–21.

47. *Time, loc. cit.* "Carnegie International" refers to "The 1958 International Exhibition of Contemporary Painting and Sculpture," Museum of Art, Carnegie Institute, Pittsburgh, Pa.

48. Rose, "Decoys and Doubles," p. 69.

49. Rose, "Graphic Work of Jasper Johns, II," p. 68.

50. Kozloff, *op. cit.,* pp. 26–27.

51. Johns told Walter Hopps: "There was a change. I don't think of it as drastic." (Hopps, *op. cit.,* p. 35.) But others did; Leo Castelli recalls that at the second Johns show, "Alfred Barr almost blanched . . . he was so disappointed. He said he didn't understand it at all."

52. This is the date suggested by Johns, and by most of the scholars of his work. There is no real reason to think he was aware of Duchamp before 1959. Attempts to get around the facts are sometimes ingenious, to say the least. Robert Pincus-Witten, in order to propose a Duchampian influence from 1955, is forced to say that "the artist's mind, unlike that of the historian, does not thrive on niggling one-to-one details. . . .": "Theater of the Conceptual: Autobiography and Myth," *Artforum,* 12, Oct. 1973, p. 42.

53. The question of whether Duchamp was working or not is the subject of considerable speculation—heightened by Duchamp himself, who enjoyed saying contradictory things. Certainly it is true that he worked in secret on *Etant donnés* during the late '60s; it was finally exhibited July 7, 1969, in the Philadelphia Museum of Art.

54. Jasper Johns, "Marcel Duchamp (1887–1968): An Appreciation," *Artforum,* 7, Nov. 1968, p. 6.

55. Kozloff, *op. cit.,* p. 29.

56. *Newsweek,* 51, March 31, 1958, p. 96.

57. "The unconscious functions satisfactorily only when the conscious mind fulfills its tasks to the very limit." C. G. Jung, "On the Nature of Dreams" (1945–48), *Dreams,* Bollingen Series XX, Princeton University Press, 1973, p. 82.

58. The idea of a 4- to 5-year period is reinforced by looking at the imagery of his painting. Thus in 1955 he did the first flags, numbers and targets; 1959, the painterly field of FALSE START and DEVICE CIRCLE; 1962–63, the tripartite canvases such as LAND'S END; 1967, the flagstone motif; 1972, the first cross-hatching.

59. I am indebted to Ken Tyler for a series of unpublished taped interviews in 1972–73 when he was at Gemini G.E.L. (He has since started his own shop, Tyler Workshops Ltd., in Bedford Village, N.Y.)

The difference in prints made during the sixties and early seventies at ULAE and Gemini can be explained in part by the difference in personalities of Mrs. Grosman and Tyler. Tatyana Grosman still maintains she knows very little about the process of printmaking, while Tyler, himself a printer, has been responsible for a number of technological innovations in the craft, including the creation of enormous prints, such as Rauschenberg's *Sky Garden* (1969).

60. Actually, it is more complicated than this. In each portfolio the edition number is signified by the appropriate numeral printed with an extra stone. That is, edition number 3 has an extra stone printed for the number three, and so on. There are also some artist's proofs with no extra stones, and for each edition, one series in which all the prints are done with two stones. See Richard S. Field, *Jasper Johns: Prints 1960–1970,* The Philadelphia Museum of Art, in conjunction with Praeger, New York, 1970, cat. nos. 17–46.

61. Tomkins, "Profile: Tatyana Grosman," p. 62.

62. "University Days," *The Thurber Carnival,* Harper & Bros., New York, 1945, p. 223.

63. Jasper Johns, "Sketchbook Notes," *Art and Literature* (Lausanne), 4, Spring 1965, p. 192 (hereafter: Johns, "Sketchbook Notes").

64. It is interesting that Johns has done American flags, but no other; American maps, but no other. The Expo '67 world MAP is evidently an anomaly.

65. Tomkins, *The Bride and the Bachelors,* p. 33.

John Cage has also been influential in his attitude toward probability as a working tool. He differs from Duchamp, at least, in his desire to use chance not only as a means of getting around the conscious mind, but the unconscious as well. This is (probably) what he means when he speaks of using chance to get rid of his own taste in music.

66. Daisetz T. Suzuki, *Zen and Japanese Culture,* Bollingen Series LXIV, Pantheon Books, New York, 1959, p. 146.

67. The stretchers are bent trapezoids but the canvas panels are not. Of this painting, Johns said, "In the painting now there is no tension. It's all an illusion." The illusion is furthered by the addition of metal plates

to join the stretcher panels together. They are not structurally necessary: "they are there to give some idea of what was happening."

68. Jerome S. Bruner, *On Knowing: Essays for the Left Hand,* Belknap Press, Cambridge, Mass., 1962, p. 24.

69. Quoted in *Sixteen Americans,* ed. Dorothy C. Miller, exhibition catalogue, The Museum of Modern Art, New York, 1959, p. 22.

70. The MAP of 1961 was done in oil, while those of 1962 and 1963 were done in encaustic, so the differences may partly reflect the differences in media.

In writing this, I cannot help recalling the comment of Kenneth Clark: "Very often in reading the description of a picture by a man of letters we feel that what the writer takes to be a stroke of dramatic genius is an accident of which the painter was quite unaware." (*Leonardo da Vinci,* Penguin, Harmondsworth, England, 1959, p. 95.) In a sense, this is inevitable. All criticism can be viewed as psychological projection, and a writer accustomed to structuring events in a dramatic form is more likely to see drama than another person. At the same time I think there is a readiness among critics of all art forms to explain things on the basis of accident. This can be very annoying, and logically ludicrous. The limiting case is perhaps film criticism.

71. Jorge Luis Borges, *Ficciones,* Grove Press, New York, 1962, p. 15. A similar thought occurs in his statement that "It is enough that a book be possible for it to exist." (*Op. cit.,* p. 85n.)

72. This, of course, leads directly to the problem of artistic intention, which has been the subject of much scholarly writing. Hoping to learn more, I read the first paragraph of an article which began (I quote it anonymously):

The approach is tripartite, each part a stage transcending its predecessor: (1) artistic intention as the matter-of-fact ground of art, in the same way in which, as Husserl describes it, the "foundation of naive-objectivistic science" is something taken for granted; (2) the subjectivization of the perception of art through the deliberate introduction of a systematic doubt of the presumably self-evident objectivity of its ground—the doubt is designed to counteract the self-evidence—issuing in a phenomenological reduction of art, which, while it complicates the occupation of creating it with a preoccupation with its origin—at times the two exist in ironic interrelation, as in Duchamp—forces "the entrance" to a radical consciousness of art, to a critical consciousness of its foundation; (3) the reviewing, under the auspices of the phenomenological epoche, of artistic intention as "that *ultimate originality* which, once apparent, *apodictically masters* the will" to create art.

73. If the relationship of the idea to the finished work is troublesome, how do we explain the artist's subjective feelings of disappointment when the work is done? These feelings are real and common. I suspect it has nothing to do with the failure to execute an imagined work; on the contrary, I think the creation is usually richer than the thought that precedes it. The disappointment is something else, and it is akin to postpartum depression (which is thought to have a hormonal basis—withdrawal of endogenous tranquilizing hormones, so we don't want to draw the analogy too closely). But there is a pleasure in creating, a kind of losing oneself, and that pleasure ceases when the work is finished. That is one reason why so many artists linger interminably over the finishing touches; they don't want to be done; they dread the depressive withdrawal.

74. Rose relates the piece to the equation of looking and eating, which is certainly a later idea expressed in Johns' notebooks—and which may be implied by his use of eating utensils in the work of the 1960s. But the antecedent story for THE CRITIC SEES seems to involve talking. In any case, the sculpture is biting; it gives us something to chew over; and we can all enjoy mouthing off about what it is saying. Or what we see it says. Or what we say it sees.

75. Rose, "Graphic Work of Jasper Johns, II," p. 65.

76. Kozloff, *op. cit.,* p. 33.

77. Johns: "The conservative treatment (of panels) is partly to do with the idea of play, showing a thing in different ways, and partly to do with my lack of invention."

78. In ARRIVE/DEPART (1963–64) there is also an impression of a skull in the lower right corner. Leo Castelli speculates: "The Sculls were important collectors of Jasper's work, but there was a disagreement, and at the time of Jasper's 1964 retrospective at the Jewish Museum, they refused to loan their pictures for the exhibit. I finally convinced them, but I think Jasper had his revenge in that painting."

79. Actually, Jim Dine had recently shaved his head, and he served as a model for the plaster cast. A rubber mask was made, and attached to a piece of wood, and painted. Johns considered the work completed, but after a few days, decided he did not like it, and destroyed it.

80. Edmund Carpenter, *Oh, What a Blow·That Phantom Gave Me!,* Holt, Rinehart & Winston, New York, 1973, p. 26.

81. Rose, "Graphic Work of Jasper Johns, II," p. 66.

82. Rudolf Virchow (1821–1902), a German nineteenth-century Renaissance man, is best remembered as a medical pathologist. He was also an anthropologist of stature, and accompanied Heinrich Schliemann to Troy in 1879. In addition he was an important liberal politician; Bismarck challenged him to a duel in 1865.

As a politician and advocate of public health, Virchow constructed Berlin's sewage system and water supply.

In pathology, Virchow discovered and named leukemia, embolism, and thrombosis; and such important structures as myelin, which sheathes nerves. His theoretical contributions to cell biology were, historically, as important as his clinical work.

Pathologists still repeat Virchow's dictum that "we see what we know," for it has practical meaning easily demonstrated. Students of pathology are treated to so-called "organ recitals"; these are conferences where healthy and diseased body parts are passed around the table for examination. It is common experience for students to stare directly at a tumor of liver or kidney and fail to see anything abnormal. The pathology is not overlooked because it is subtle; even quite striking changes remain invisible to the naive observer. Once the pathology is pointed out, the student is often amazed he was unable to see it before, and he can immediately recognize it in future examples.

83. Hart Crane, *The Bridge,* Horace Liveright, New York, 1930, p. 46.

84. Jung, "The Practical Use of Dream Analysis" (1934), *op. cit.,* p. 93.

85. There are actually two paintings, SOUVENIR and SOUVENIR 2.

86. Johns, "Sketchbook Notes," pp. 185–92.

87. The bravest attempt is that of Richard S. Field, *op. cit.*

88. The painting was done in Japan, and Johns had great difficulty finding in that country a chair with sufficiently long legs.

89. Rose, "Decoys and Doubles," p. 72.

90. John Cage, "26 Statements re Duchamp," *Art and Literature* (Lausanne), 3, Autumn–Winter 1964, p. 9.

91. Johns' sketchbook notes contain the following comment: "Simplification occurs not because one 'wants' it—but because one thing is not another thing. (Leonardo's *Deluge* drawings.) There is the business of approximation—what we hope is that anything meaning another thing will have a 'life' of its own, free from that other thing. The thing which 'means' has strengths (?) which are not dependent upon what is meant."

92. John Ashbery, "Art and Artists," *New York Herald Tribune (European Edition),* June 28, 1961.

93. *Idem,* "Paris Notes," *Art International* (Lugano), 6, Dec. 20, 1962, p. 51.

94. *Newsweek,* 61, Feb. 18, 1963, p. 65.

95. Dore Ashton, "Art," *Arts and Architecture,* 80, March 1963, p. 6.

96. Tillim, *op. cit.,* pp. 22, 25.

97. *Time,* 87, Jan. 14, 1965, p. 71.

98. The device of the imprint is also carried through with the circular paint can, from PASSAGE II (1966), through CORPSE AND MIRROR (1974) and other paintings.

99. Two notebook entries consider this question: What does it mean?
    "There are differences but they are not noticed."
    And again:
    Making distinctions where
        None has existed
        None has been said to exist
        None has been made

100. Lawrence Alloway, "Art," *The Nation,* 213, Nov. 22, 1971, p. 541.

101. The exception is the stone for FIGURE 9, which cracked in the original black series printing, and had to be redrawn.

102. This is literally true; at the bottom of the print the row of little Johnsian images represents etching-plate images used some years before, and reproduced here.

103. Mark Lancaster read an early draft of this manuscript and pointed out that I had "read" the painting from right to left. The painting contains no such directions. I am perplexed on this point because at one time I asked Johns whether he thought people would have a different experience of the painting depending on their written linguistic tradition—that is, English is read left to right, Arabic is right to left, and Japanese is vertical, and so on. I thought there might be a tendency to read in the ordinary direction of the eye's travel. Apparently I have answered my own question.

104. *Dictionnaire abrégé du surréalisme,* quoted in André Breton, *Surrealism and Painting,* Icon Editions, Harper & Row, New York, 1972, p. 289.

105. The mirror is canceled, as a printing plate—which of course produces a reversed image—is canceled, with a large X.

106. *The National Geographic Magazine,* 143, May 1973, p. 668.

107. ". . . to conceal . . . [he] had resorted to the comprehensive and sagacious expedient of not attempting to conceal it at all." Auguste Dupin, speaking of "The Purloined Letter" (1845), in Poe, *op. cit.,* p. 306.

108. *Foirades/Fizzles,* Petersburg Press, New York (etchings printed by Atelier Crommelynck, Paris), 1976. (Five texts by Samuel Beckett; thirty-three original etchings by Jasper Johns.)

109. John Cage, "Jasper Johns: Stories and Ideas," in *Jasper Johns,* exhibition catalogue, The Jewish Museum, New York, 1964, p. 21.

110. Rose, "Graphic Work of Jasper Johns, II," p. 74.

3.

The Function of
THE OBSERVER

In a celebrated remark, Marcel Duchamp said "it is the spectators who make the pictures." He meant by this that a work of art stands at a sort of midpoint between creator and viewer, and that each contributes to it. What the work of art means, how it is perceived, and literally *what it is* become not only a function of the artist's action but the viewer's response.

Jasper Johns shares this attitude. The viewer's participation is implied in all his work, and it is made explicit in his TARGET (1960), where the spectator is invited to complete the image, and to sign his name alongside the artist. It is a characteristic of Johns' work: self-contained (the artist provides all the materials for the interaction); simple (evoking of childish play, coloring books); and literal in a way that undercuts the profound implications it carries.

But the idea of participating in a work of art troubles many viewers, even critics. Lawrence Alloway says that "Johns has conceded to the spectator the right to determine the meaning of his works,"[1] as if there were an alternative. In fact there is no alternative. An artist cannot fix his meanings absolutely, even if he wanted to do so. Art functions in the region of indeterminate or ambiguous meanings, and always has. But modern art, and particularly the work of Jasper Johns, exaggerates this ambiguity, and plays upon our modern understanding of the observer's crucial role in determining the nature of reality. It is that role, and that experience, which must be explored.

The task of the spectator is to decide what he is looking at. How is this done? We have some insight in a reaction to Jasper Johns' first show in 1958. Leo Steinberg has written with sensitive introspection:

> My own first reaction was normal. I disliked the show, and would gladly have thought it a bore. . . . I was angry at the artist, as if he had invited me to a meal, only to serve something uneatable. . . . I was irritated at some of my friends for pretending to like it—but with an uneasy suspicion that perhaps they did like it, so that I was really mad at myself for being so dull, and at the whole situation for showing me up.[2]

Steinberg summarized his reaction as "bewildered alarm." He expressed anxiety, uneasiness, the feeling of uncertainty about where he stands:

> I am challenged to estimate the aesthetic value of, say, a drawer stuck into a canvas. But nothing I've ever seen can teach me how this is to be done. I am alone with this thing, and it is up to me to evaluate it in the absence of available standards.[3]

Nearly twenty years after this show, Steinberg's response now seems overdramatic. We have already lost sight of certain qualities of the early flags, numbers, and targets which were perceived as startling and shocking. Alfred Barr would not buy FLAG (1955) from the first show for the Museum of Modern Art, fearing patriotic repercussions; and TARGET WITH PLASTER CASTS (1955) had been turned down by both the Jewish Museum and the Modern because the casts included genitalia. These were significant points

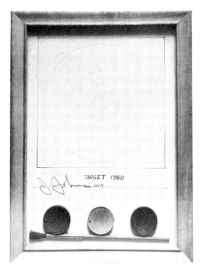

TARGET. 1960. Pencil on board with brush and watercolor disks, 17.1 x 11.8 cm (16¾ x 4⅝"). Private collection

TARGET WITH FOUR FACES. 1955. Encaustic and collage on canvas with objects, 75.5 x 66 cm (29¾ x 26"). The Museum of Modern Art, New York. Gift of Mr. and Mrs. Robert Scull

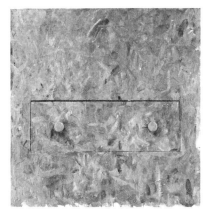

DRAWER. 1957. See Plate 14

in the late 1950s; they guided people's actions. Today those fears seem quaint, almost endearing.

But Steinberg is not reacting from outraged patriotism or modesty; his response is more fundamental. He is looking at a group of paintings which do not conform to his ideas of what a painting is, or what it should be. They cannot be fitted into any mental category he possesses. They break with convention. And in this sense, Steinberg's bewildered alarm is no different from the reaction of thousands of art observers in the past when first confronted by something that is genuinely new.

His initial reaction was modified with familiarity and later thought. But one aspect of the observer's response to Johns' work remains: "I am alone with this thing, and it is up to me to evaluate it. . . ." A person looking at Johns' work often feels *alone* in an odd way. This is in part a reflection of Johns' own isolated personality, and in part a modern dilemma of epistemology which Johns re-creates—the dilemma of the observer looking out at the world and trying to make sense of it.

For more than three centuries, "sense" in the Western world has increasingly meant scientific sense. Since the time of Galileo, we have come to believe in an objective, independently verifiable reality, to be investigated, measured, and controlled through science.

The scientific method advanced lives, wealth, and knowledge. Its introduction coincided with the Renaissance, the discovery of the New World, and the rise of capitalist nation-states. Science provided increasingly the method men used to think and act, until it replaced religion almost entirely as the accepted framework from which to view the world.

The fundamental feature of science was that its method canceled out the prejudices of the observer. If Galileo dropped two weights and found they landed together, why, so could anyone else, and obtain the same result. The age, sex, nationality, or religious persuasion of the observer was irrelevant—it did not affect the outcome. A scientific experiment was not a matter of opinion; it was much more tangible than that, more real. And while there were disputes, they were not like theological disputes in the Middle Ages. Scientific disputes could be resolved, and were. Science was a practical technique.

The limitations of science became evident only very slowly. In 1623, Galileo announced exuberantly, "Nature is written in mathematical language."[4] He meant it literally; nature is mathematical in the same way the sky is blue. However, by 1899, Bertrand Russell had a different view: "Physics is mathematical not because we know so much about the physical world, but because we know so little: it is only its mathematical properties that we can discover."[5] One is reminded of Abraham Maslow's comment that if all you have is a hammer, you tend to treat everything as if it were a nail.

Because science could only deal with verifiable, repeatable phenomena, only these were studied. Other events, and other ways of looking at the world, were ignored or said to be impossible. The trouble with these other views was that they required a change in the positions of the objective observer, dispassionately looking at objective reality. Nowhere was this objective observer more important than in physics.

Physics was the first "hard" science. It was the first to be mathematical, the first to shatter theological belief systems, the first to produce a grave moral crisis for its practitioners. So it is not surprising that physics was the first field to come up squarely against the limitations imposed by the idea of the objective observer.

Einstein struck the first blow with his special theory of relativity in 1905. Relativity destroyed the concept of the stable, objective observer. The idea that two independent people could perform the same experiment and get the same result was no longer a certainty. On the contrary, Einstein showed that in many situations two observers would see things very differently, and their instruments would record differently.

The next wrenching came with quantum physics in the period from 1900 to 1930. Quantum theory is not a single idea, nor is it associated with a single physicist. It emerged from a series of difficult and paradoxical problems. In 1900, Max Planck concluded that radiant energy—such as light—exists in the form of discrete packets, or quanta. In 1913, Niels Bohr demonstrated that the idea of the quantum had to be applied to the structure of atoms, as well. Ernest Rutherford had proposed that the atom was like a miniature solar system; around a heavy center of protons and neutrons, lightweight electrons spun in different orbits. But Bohr said these orbits were fixed in a quantum way. George Gamow draws the analogy to an automobile gear box—you can drive in first, second, or third gear, but not anywhere in between.[6]

This makes quantum theory sound definite, but in fact it was the indefinite, statistical aspects of the theory that made it controversial. To carry Gamow's analogy a step further, in observing cars on a road you may know they are all in one gear or another, but you cannot know in which gear any particular car is at any particular time. To describe one car, or all the cars together, one is forced to make statistical statements. The idea that the universe was fundamentally statistical did not sit well with many physicists. Einstein was adamant that "God does not throw dice"—to which Bohr replied: "Nor is it our business to prescribe to God how he should run the world."

The paradoxes inherent in statistical descriptions became more pronounced with time, and quantum explanations became increasingly divorced from "common sense."[7] Eventually we find Robert Oppenheimer speaking of atomic structure this way:

If we ask, for instance, whether the position of the electron remains the same, we must say "no"; if we ask whether the electron's position changes with time, we must say "no"; if we ask whether the electron is at rest, we must say "no"; if we ask whether it is in motion, we must say "no."[8]

This places the role of the observer in considerable confusion. The old dualities—it's there or it isn't, it happened or it didn't—no longer apply.

No (detail). 1961. See Plate 80

What, then, is the observer doing?

Werner Heisenberg provided one answer with the Uncertainty Principle in 1927. At that time, physicists were exploring the atom by firing particles at atomic nuclei, and knocking off other particles. They were trying to measure the mass and direction of the ejected particles, and having trouble. Heisenberg conclusively demonstrated that it couldn't be done—if you measured mass, you altered direction, and if you measured direction, you changed the mass.[9]

The Uncertainty Principle was disturbing because it showed there was something you couldn't know—something you could never know. It was a clear limit to the scientific method, because in order to observe, the observer had to interfere with the event, and change its outcome. One could not make the observation in a neutral, uninvolved way.

In the following years, the quest for fundamental particles continued, using larger and more powerful particle accelerators—"atom smashers"— to pour more and more energy into the splitting process. But this search for the fundamental building blocks of the universe has, after more than 75 years, taken an unexpected turn. There are now over 200 "fundamental" particles, and still others are discovered each year.

Many of these new particles owe their existence to the enormous quantities of energy the physicists are applying in their experiments. In other words, the new particles aren't being discovered—they're being created.[10] They are not artifacts of nature, but of man.

Thus the culmination of nearly a century of scientific inquiry into the nature of the universe yields, in the end, only a reflection of the observer and his methods. The results tell us more about ourselves than they do about the universe; we find, not objective reality, but a kind of mirror of our preoccupations. The question determines the answer.

Modern physicists seem to accept this. It is implicit in their terminology. Two generations ago physicists gave their discoveries pristine Greek and Latin names worthy of Linnaeus—proton, electron, quantum. But their modern counterparts indulge a personal, even idiosyncratic taxonomy which refers more to the physicist than to the particle. In 1953 the quality of "strangeness" was invoked to explain the strange fact that some particles survived longer than expected. In 1964 "charm" was postulated because it would be charming if a particle with this quality were found. James Joyce's *Finnegans Wake* provided the name for the current candidate for the fundamental unit of nature—the quark. In 1976, the Nobel Prize was awarded to the discoverers of a quark/anti-quark particle which possessed hidden charm, as opposed to naked charm. And there is now talk of new particles with qualities of "truth" and "beauty."

It would be simple to dismiss this terminology as self-indulgent. Its implications may run deeper. Shakespeare said "Nothing is, but thinking makes it so," a sentiment generally appreciated for its psychological validity. But in 1930 James Jeans wrote:

The universe begins to look more like a great thought than like a great machine. Mind no longer appears as an accidental intruder into the realm of matter; we are beginning to suspect that we ought rather to hail it as the creator and governor of the realm of matter. . . .[11]

Can this really be meant literally? John Wheeler skitters around the idea:

Nothing is more important about the quantum principle than this, that it destroys the concept of the world as "sitting out there," with the observer safely separated from it by a 20-centimeter slab of plate glass. Even to observe so minuscule an object as an electron, he must shatter the glass. He must reach in. He must install his chosen measuring equipment. It is up to him to decide whether he shall measure position or momentum. To install the equipment to measure the one prevents and excludes his installing the equipment to measure the other. Moreover, the measurement changes the state of the electron. The universe will never afterwards be the same. To describe what has happened, one has to cross out that old word "observer" and put in its place the new word "participator." In some strange sense the universe is a participatory universe.[12]

Wheeler then asks the hard question: "Are we, in the words of Thomas Mann 'actually bringing about what seems to be happening'? Are we destined to return to the deep conception of Parmenides . . . that, 'what is, . . . is identical with the thought that recognizes it'?"

Here we find the idea that "the spectator makes the pictures" raised in a new and astonishing context. Do physicists make the universe? It is more comfortable to back off to Heisenberg's idea, that what we observe is not nature itself, but nature "exposed to our method of questioning,"[13] the earlier notion that our conceptions of nature are not to be confused with nature itself; that the map is not the territory;[14] that any representation of reality is, in the end, no more than a representation—a stand-in, a surrogate, a tool, a way of thinking.

Map. 1962. Encaustic and collage on canvas, 152.4 x 236.2 cm (60 x 93″). Collection Mr. and Mrs. Frederick R. Weisman, Beverly Hills, California

But we may summarize the recent history of physics as leading to a crisis of the observer—as he has been moved from an objective witness to a relative witness, as his knowledge is obtained only by interfering with the event he studies, and as, finally, he creates the event itself, so that observer and observed are inextricably linked. The study of physics has turned more and more into the study of physicists—which, one can argue, is all it ever was in the first place.

"Artists," says Kenneth Clark, ". . . have always responded instinctively to latent assumptions about the shape of the universe."[15] It is worth tracing briefly how Western artists have incorporated these assumptions in their work, particularly assumptions about the role of the observer.

Renaissance painters, living in a kind of protoscientific environment, a world where exact measurement of objective reality was yielding powerful new insights, were naturally drawn to attempt scientific painting. The most notable result was the innovation of linear perspective. Perspective could be described in a set of rules, or laws, for the representation of space and volume; it was scientific, geometric, mathematical, precise—in short, it gave

Land's End (detail). 1963. See Plate 100

to painting a method that conformed, in intention, to the intellectual principles of the day.

Arnold Hauser observes that "only since the Renaissance has painting been based on the assumption that the space in which things exist is an infinite, continuous and homogeneous element, and that we usually see things uniformly, that is to say, with a single and motionless eye."[16] This is a perfect description of the space conception of classical Newtonian physics, and a perfect description of the idealized Newtonian observer, who watches with a single motionless eye.

Renaissance space turned the picture frame into a window, through which one looked onto an imagined scene. The position of the observer was fixed. The painting told him where he stood—and he stood outside, looking in. The Renaissance spectator was not a participator in the picture, but a passive watcher. He did not influence the picture; he did not interact with it. The artist painted, and the observer looked on.

For the next four hundred years, the position of the observer remained essentially unchanged. Post-Renaissance artists bent and modified spatial conventions, without departing from the Renaissance ideal that the painter should represent what is actually seen. They used light and shadow, tone and color to expand their possibilities in depicting the visual world. There was never any real break with Renaissance conventions; Leonardo's notebooks contain many ideas which were still being explored by the Impressionists several centuries later. The ideal of the objective observer was never questioned.

Picasso. *Les Demoiselles d'Avignon*. 1907.
The Museum of Modern Art, New York.
Acquired through the Lillie P. Bliss Bequest

Dissatisfactions began to appear after 1860, and they can be seen in new spatial conventions. Edouard Manet caused his paintings to be flat; Paul Cézanne introduced distorted, "peripheral" perspective as an ordinary feature of his work. As we will see later, these changes are best explained as an insight into the nature of representation, but they certainly paralleled a new scientific uncertainty about "objective reality."

A break-point comes in the early twentieth century. Picasso's *Les Demoiselles d'Avignon* was painted in 1907, two years after Einstein's special relativity theory, and the painting can be considered the first document of Cubism.

Cubism is a conceptual art, which does not pretend any longer to reproduce the world as we see it. If Guillaume Apollinaire speaks for the Cubists, then the link between scientific advances and painting conventions is made explicit in 1913: "Today, the scientists do not confine themselves to the three dimensions of Euclidean geometry. Naturally and by intuition the painters were also led to the point where they concern themselves with new means of extension. . . ."[17]

Cubism did not destroy perspective, it merely multiplied it. But by doing so, it displaced the observer from his comfortable, fixed position. It was no longer so easy to enter the picture through the canvas window; the question of the artist's intent, the difficulty of following his vision, became barriers. The fact that the picture was only a representation of reality—a trace remaining of the artist's own complex vision—was all too obvious.

Just as physicists were discovering that their fields of inquiry had more to

Georges Braque. *Man with a Guitar*. 1911.
The Museum of Modern Art, New York.
Acquired through the Lillie P. Bliss Bequest

do with themselves than with any objective reality, so artists were increasingly devoted to the idea of art as a self-contained system with no referents outside itself. The proper subject of art became the artist and his actions. If audiences didn't like this, if they felt left out, it was just too bad.

As the artist's own role gained importance, it was inevitable that someone would claim an ordinary object as a work of art, simply because he was an artist, and said it was. The problems caused by such an action are exemplified by Marcel Duchamp's Ready-mades.

Similarly, the trend toward increasing abstraction was inevitable. In his search for purer self-expression, the artist abandoned distracting elements, until finally representation itself—a recognizable image—was eliminated as unnecessary to the proper functioning of the artist. After all, art has always been an artificial manifestation of perceived reality. Why not just admit that, and create a completely artificial, abstract image that didn't pretend to be anything else?

That, of course, was done. Before an Abstract Expressionist painting, the objective observer—the Renaissance witness—cannot function at all. In a real sense, the observer is no longer the audience but the artist himself. As in physics, the observer and the observed are inextricably linked. And as in physics, this linkage produces a language of personal, internal reference which the outsider finds obscure and forbidding.

But just as physics would come to a standstill if there were no fresh experiments—new inquiries into the physical world—to ponder and explain, so art would cease to function if it divorced itself entirely from the perceptual world. From this point of view, complete abstraction represents a kind of limiting case for art; it cannot exist except in opposition to a tradition of representational art. The decline of Abstract Expressionism can be seen as a logical consequence of its international acceptance. One could argue that the movement was too successful for its own good; by demolishing alternatives it diminished its own power. In another context, Anton Ehrenzweig observes:

> Any innovation necessarily disrupts existing sensibilities. But the surrealistic spirit of modern art went out of its way to twist our rational sensibilities and attack our reason. What may have happened in the second half of the twentieth century is that this deliberate twisting no longer excites. . . . Modern art was based largely on surrealist techniques of surprise and disruption. . . . They have lost all meaning. Possibly art . . . will have to revert to more constructive, intellectually controlled techniques, which nevertheless do not exclude the participation of the unconscious.[18]

It is Jasper Johns' peculiar gift that he was able to assimilate the advances and developments of twentieth-century art, and to shift the experience of the observer away from the painter and back to the audience. Not surprisingly, audiences have responded with pleasure and gratitude, even though the dilemmas he presents are troublesome.

How did he do this? We have already noted that he re-introduced the

Marcel Duchamp. *In Advance of the Broken Arm.* 1915. Yale University Art Gallery, New Haven. Gift of Katherine S. Dreier to the Collection Société Anonyme

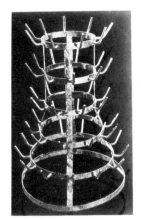

Marcel Duchamp. *Bottle Rack.*
1914. Collection Estate of
Man Ray, Paris

PAINTED BRONZE. 1960. See Plate 67

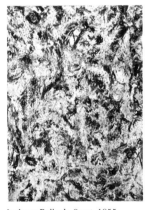

Jackson Pollock. *Scent.* 1955.
Collection Mr. and Mrs.
Frederick R. Weisman, Beverly Hills, California

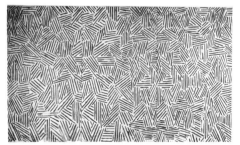

SCENT. 1973–74. See Plate 161

recognizable image, representation, into modern art. But he did so in a peculiar way. Johns has a talent for insinuating himself into spaces where there does not, at first, seem to be room for play. In terms of conventional art history, we could simplify his stance and say that he has slipped in between Duchamp and Pollock, between the found object and the created abstraction.

In doing so, he often seems to reverse or invert the attitudes of his predecessors. Thus Duchamp took a bottle rack and called it his own; Johns patiently builds two ale cans in the most complicated way imaginable, expending great effort on almost reproducing an ordinary object. Pollock's last painting, *Scent,* shows an abstraction born of spontaneity and freedom; Johns' image of the same title (SCENT, 1973–74) is equally abstract, but carried upon an elaborately worked-out symmetry, which is mathematical in its precision—and ultimately the reverse of real spontaneity.

There is a certain interest in relating Johns' work to the ordered stream of images that constitutes art history. Johns himself is careful to provoke such considerations; he builds an historical sense into the implied meaning of his pictures.

But there is a deeper question about Johns, and a more fundamentally interesting one. Ehrenzweig suggests it when he speaks of "the participation of the unconscious." Johns is an artist who has chosen, through all his working life, to put himself squarely at the junction of abstraction and representation. His work always seems to oscillate between the thing and the representation of the thing. By doing this, he engages the most significant questions of art, as an activity of human beings. People who know nothing about art somehow smell this in his work, and are drawn to it. And since he is an artist with such a careful sense of history, we are obliged to review a few aspects of the history of representation in art.

The earliest Western art—the cave paintings of Spain and in the Dordogne valley of France—is associated with anatomically modern man, beginning about 30,000 years ago. The Cro-Magnon artists were hunters, and their drawings center on animals and the activity of the hunt.

Most authorities ascribe a function of sympathetic magic to this cave art—animals were represented to increase their number, or to invoke success in future hunts. Thus visual art began as an attempt to influence the future course of human activity in the natural world. If man is a tool-making animal—and if tools are man's way to control the environment—then art was first seen as still another manual tool to subdue nature. To make a representation on a cave wall was to alter the outcome of events in time.

This implies a belief about representation that has never been lost, even to the present day. We smile when superstitious people refuse to let tourists take their picture; but on television a woman sharpshooter declined to shoot out the eyes of photographs of her children;[19] in anger we tear up the picture of a person who displeases us—and then we feel guilty, as if we have actually harmed the person. On some primitive level we all retain the idea—thousands of years old—that the image of the thing itself is tied to the thing itself, and that what we do to the image is done to the thing it represents.

Yet there is another feature of representation which is also very old—the conflict between the attributes of a thing and the necessity to represent it in a static image. The device of a multi-legged creature to convey a running beast may be the first representational convention in Western art.

Altamira. The Painted Ceiling

Thus, in our minds a picture stands for something beyond the picture. But the picture itself is made according to techniques which must be considered conventional. These two aspects of representation are not contradictory. Quite the reverse—the emotional impact of representation is always carried in the conventions of the day even if this fact is not immediately apparent.

A pictorial convention is, of course, arbitrary.[20] Its meaning is learned; once assimilated, the convention tends to become "invisible," and we may even begin to think of it as a feature of reality itself.

For example, most ordinary viewers expect to see a picture which suggests depth by the mechanism of linear perspective. A viewer often says that such a painting "looks real," or that it "looks like the way things really are." But such a belief is only a few hundred years old. Perspective was an innovation of the Renaissance, as we have noted. What is less widely recognized is that when it was first introduced, a painting in perspective looked peculiar and subjective. It certainly did not look like the way things really were.

Prior to that time, the use of painted space was very different. It was perfectly reasonable to show two incidents from one story in the same picture; time was not respected. It was also reasonable to show objects in space as they were known to be, and not merely as they appeared.

The Renaissance changed all that. In perspective, a moment in time and a position in space were firmly fixed. It became illogical and "unscientific" to paint in any other fashion. After centuries of familiarity, perspective has come to look real to us, in a way that Gothic or Byzantine conventions do not. But perspective is still a convention, and early Renaissance painters knew it:

Nardo di Cione. *Hell.* 1350s. Strozzi Chapel, Sta. Maria Novella, Florence

> For a long time, a strong undercurrent of doubt and ambiguity (so welcome to the symbolic form play of the depth mind) must still have run on underneath a growing appreciation of the laws of perspective. . . . One feels how in the first exuberant experiments with perspective during the early Renaissance, the double meaning of perspective must have lain still nearer to the surface and how the artists must have made an almost conscious use of it. . . . We know that depth perception projects a sexual symbolism into any part of the human body. . . . It was no longer necessary to depict the various parts of the body in their "real" and "constant" size and proportions. Any limb could be lengthened, shortened, or contorted to express a hidden symbolism (for instance, of castration).[21]

Ehrenzweig adds: "The 'discovery' of perspective is hailed as a rational

Paolo Uccello. *Battle of San Romano*
(detail). c. 1445.
Uffizi Gallery, Florence

Leonardo da Vinci. *Annunciation.*
Late 1470s. Uffizi Gallery, Florence

Melozzo da Forlì.
The Angel of the Annunciation.
Before 1480. Uffizi Gallery,
Florence

Study for WALL PIECE. 1968–69.
Graphite, gouache, ink, and collage on paper,
74.7 x 93.3 cm (29⅜ x 36¾").
Collection Kimiko and John Powers, Colorado

achievement of art enriching our knowledge of nature. Psychologically, it is nothing of the sort."[22]

Whether one accepts this Freudian view of the power of perspective, it is certainly true that its function in painting was quickly turned to purposes that can hardly be explained as attempts at realism. Paolo Uccello produced the *Battle of San Romano* (c. 1445) in the early days of perspective experimentation. To modern eyes, it is easy to see that illusory depth and flatness compete; the kicking horse exists both as an abstract painted shape and as a visual cue suggesting depth; we perceive both at once.

Leonardo's early, sometimes-disputed *Annunciation* (late 1470s) gives a convincing illusion of depth. Now perspective is more subtly employed, through the disposition of the figures—the angel appearing in profile, the Virgin almost full-face. There is a psychological and sexual meaning to the orientation of the human face in space.[23] Furthermore, Leonardo set the angel against a natural landscape, and the Virgin against a jutting building with sharp man-made angles. Here one feels that perspective largely determines the impact of the whole.[24]

Finally, there is the remarkable perspective of Mantegna's *Dead Christ* (after 1466). The painting is noteworthy because its perspective is simply wrong, according to the mathematical rules. You cannot align this painting toward a single fixed vanishing point; its perspectives are mixed, and closer to those of Cézanne than any Renaissance artist.

This "error" by Mantegna, an acknowledged master of perspective, clearly produces a powerful emotional statement. In fact, conventions—since they are invisible—always serve as carriers of emotional content. Unless we accept this, certain preoccupations make little sense. Renaissance artists were fascinated with the human form draped in robes. Painters wrote at length on the various ways of portraying folds, and many pictures show figures whose garments fall in such elaborate folds that this aspect of the painting seems more important than any other. And perhaps it is. Certainly there is a level of abstraction in representational works to which the eye unconsciously responds. Melozzo da Forlì's *Angel of the Annunciation* (before 1480)—with a skirt so suggestive of Johns' flagstones—makes one wonder whether "realism" was ever a consideration for the artist as he went about his work.[25]

Between observation and representation there stands a selective act, an act that requires thought. All painters are aware of it, even if their understanding is muddled. Leonardo said, "The painter who draws merely by . . . eye, without any reason, is like a mirror which copies all the things placed in front of it without being conscious of their existence."[26] His notebook entries on painting focus either on exact, detailed observations of nature, or on what we would now call *ideas:* ways to represent a battle, ways to suggest emotions in a figure, infirmity of old age, and so on. Leonardo stated the need for careful observation; but at the same time, a painting is not a mirror; something else is involved.

Renaissance perspective was followed by a succession of experiments directed at painting other things the eye sees; the subtleties of color, shadow, the play of light. Through all this, there is the insistence, by the artists themselves, that they are painting nature as it is, with increasing accuracy and subtlety. Claude Monet, for example, had "a horror of theories," and always said his own paintings were taken directly from nature, that any disparity between the perceived reality and the painted re-creation was inadvertent: "I am simply expending my efforts upon a maximum of appearances in close correlation with unknown realities. When one is on the plane of concordant appearances one cannot be far from reality, or at least from what we can know of it. . . ."[27]

Monet's attitude may stand for the majority of Western painters since the Renaissance. But there are some dissident figures in this history of artistic fidelity of nature. The first of importance is Edouard Manet, the well-to-do Parisian dandy, the artist famous for his waistcoats, his delicate women, his luminous light. In Manet's work from the 1860s onward, one can find parallels to the work of Jasper Johns a century later.

Manet was a precursor of Impressionism, a major movement to which he stood in uneasy relationship—as Johns does to Pop Art. Manet, like Johns, was notable for his willingness to let a painting be flat, lacking the illusion of depth. Courbet said that Manet's pictures were as flat as playing cards. Manet did not seem to care, although he often rationalized this flatness, as in his 1868 portrait of Zola, and especially in the 1881–82 painting *A Bar at the Folies Bergères* in which a barmaid stands before a mirror, itself of course flat. Similarly Johns chooses imagery which defuses or explains away the impact of flatness.

Like Johns, Manet needed to use pre-existing imagery as a condition of his creativity. He borrowed the compositions of old masters and even recent artists, such as Delacroix. To the astonishment of his contemporaries, Manet did not seem to think that he was "copying"; nor did he care for the precious illusionistic space behind the canvas. His concerns lay elsewhere, as do those of Johns.

Paul Cézanne, the cantankerous provincial, did not share Claude Monet's horror of theories; indeed he said that Monet was "only an eye, but my God, what an eye!"

Only an eye: even as praise, the words mark the beginning of the end for what Duchamp would later dismiss as "retinal art." Cézanne himself broke with Impressionistic philosophy even as he adopted certain of their techniques. Cézanne wanted something more permanent in his art, something of the essence of the subjects he portrayed; and his ideas set the stage for Cubism and other modern movements which increasingly did not care to represent things merely as the eye saw them.

Cézanne said of his own work: "I have not tried to reproduce nature; I have represented her." For him, this meant a departure from the Impressionistic idea of a re-creation of some fleeting, instantaneous reality; he sought a more permanent quality, even at the expense of fidelity to nature. His work is a record of his growing independence from fidelity to nature.

Edouard Manet. *A Bar at the Folies Bergères.* 1881–82. Courtauld Institute of Art, London

One can make too much of the newness of all this. In fact, the interpretive act—the middle ground between what is seen and what is shown—was always important. It is a consequence of the way history works that we no longer sense it so clearly in old paintings.[28]

For example, only a handful of Renaissance Annunciations have come down to us, and of these most are now sanctified by a museum setting and centuries of praise. We have long since lost the ability to feel the religious emotion once evoked by the image; and we have certainly lost the ability to see these few Annunciations in the hundreds of other portrayals of the scene. We no longer perceive the Renaissance artist as shackled to a repertoire of subject matter and stock imagery which had stood for centuries, and which he was now obliged to show freshly—an almost impossible task. We have forgotten that Renaissance painters rarely chose their subjects; their patrons did that, and patrons were as conservative then as they are now. They called for standard Biblical incidents, and the artist was judged by his ability to make the familiar new, and wondrous, and wonderful.

Renaissance artists went about their business by presenting a new, "scientific" view of reality. But this should not delude us into thinking anything was really changed.

The interpretive act, hidden behind the rhetoric of representation, remained as important as ever. One can argue that the technique of the Impressionists was a bold interpretive stance, even as their avowed philosophy maintained that there was no philosophy, except to show what was. In Monet's later work, the brushy color fields approach abstraction; many images cannot be "read" close up.

Cézanne's brush strokes serve as a design element that competes, in a sense, with the overall composition. This is clearly seen in pictures such as *The Banks of the Marne* (1888). Another feature of Cézanne's work is his liberal treatment of perspective. It has been much discussed as a more "accurate" perspective of peripheral vision; we need only note that in pictures such as *Portrait of Gustave Geffroy* (1895)—where the table slopes so precipitously that the open books must fall to the floor—the old Renaissance ideas are ignored.

Cézanne was aware of what he was doing; he notes: "There are two things in the painter, the eye and the brain. The two must cooperate; one must work for the development of both . . . : of the eye through the outlook on nature, of the brain through the logic of organized sensations which provide the means of expression."[29]

The eye and the brain have continued as poles of complementary force throughout art history. Twentieth-century art can be simply described as the ascendancy of the brain over the eye.

The eye, wrote Leonardo, sees all objects reversed. Johannes Kepler, writing in 1604, compared the eye to a darkened chamber, or "camera," and said: "Vision is brought about by pictures of the thing seen being formed on the white concave surface of the retina." René Descartes actually took the eye of an ox, scraped the back to make it transparent, and set it in a hole in a

Paul Cézanne. *The Banks of the Marne* (detail). 1888. The Hermitage Museum, Leningrad

Paul Cézanne. *Portrait of Gustave Geffroy.* 1895. Collection Mme René Lecomte, Paris

darkened room, so that he could see the small inverted image of the scene outside.

Since then, the eye as a camera has become a textbook platitude. There is some truth to it. The eye does function like a camera; but vision is a far different matter.

In the first place, we do not see what is projected onto the back of our eyeballs. Only a small area, the fovea, can perceive sharply; the rest of the image is a sort of colorful blur. We are able to bring a whole scene in focus by rapid eye movements, exposing our fovea to different parts of the incoming image; but this means that the scene we see before us is a composite image, built up over time.

Second, the composite retinal image is immediately transformed in terms of information. There are approximately 10,000,000 nerve cells in each retina—but the optic nerve connecting the eye to the brain has only 250,000 fibers. Clearly, complex data-processing has already occurred before the electrical impulses of sight ever reach the brain to be interpreted.[30]

Third, this interpretation by the cortex is extremely complicated. We tend to think of it as natural—look at something, recognize it, and say what it is—but in fact it requires learning. People having congenital cataracts, who are enabled by surgery to see for the first time as adults, cannot at first distinguish between a circle and a square. Later they can tell the difference, but can't say what the difference is. Not until they verbalize concepts such as line, angle, and curve, are they able to articulate what they see.

There is abundant evidence for the importance of learning on simple perception. In one Swiftian experiment, it was shown that cats raised in an environment of horizontal lines would later walk into the legs of a chair; cats raised in a vertical environment would avoid the chair legs, but would never jump up onto the horizontal seat.[31]

In more complicated ways, what we see is related to what we have already seen. Memory can be thought of as a kind of stored perception, which we use to help us interpret new events in our world. In addition, the ability to verbalize and the ability to act are related to perception. Injuries to portions of the brain may produce a variety of disruptions in the way we respond to the visual world. A patient, given a toothbrush, may be able to identify it, but not to use it—or to use it, but not state its name—or to hear the word "toothbrush" and describe the article, but not recognize it when shown, and so on.

Sketch for The Critic Smiles. 1959. Charcoal on paper, 13 x 21.6 cm (5⅛ x 8½"). Collection the artist

Thus perception is not the passive process it was thought to be two hundred years ago. Perception has nothing to do with the eye as a camera; we do not "see" the images on the backs of our eyeballs. Instead, what we see is the result of an active, inquisitive search of our environment, and an active, intellectual process of assigning learned meanings to the information we gather. The fact that we are unaware of this continuous effort does not make it any less real.

It has been estimated that 90 percent of all the information we receive about the world comes to us through our eyes. We transform that information,

FRAGMENT—ACCORDING TO WHAT—BENT "BLUE."
1971. Lithograph, 64.8 x 73 cm (25½ x 28¾").
Published by Gemini G.E.L.

René Magritte. *The Promenades of Euclid*
(Les Promenades d'Euclide). 1955.
The Minneapolis Institute of Arts

Single frame from Shower Scene
of Alfred Hitchcock's *Psycho*

taking what is useful to us and ignoring the rest. In doing so, we often see only what we want to see; this is a very old idea. Helmholtz spoke of perception as "unconscious inferences."[32]

The need for continuity in interpreting our sensory world is met at the expense of divergent or contradictory information which we ignore—which we will often fight hard not to see. But there must always be a considerable tension in our perceptual apparatus, a tension that comes from the awareness, at some level, of what we are consciously ignoring. From time to time, that tension can be collapsed, and in a moment of surprise we become aware of what has been ignored.

Most commonly, tension is collapsed through art which deals with ambiguous information. The best art always sets our eyes and our brains at war in some way which must be resolved. Ordinarily that resolution invokes the unconscious mind.

We have suggested that Jasper Johns involves the unconscious mind of the observer in his art. How is this done? It is a critical cliché to say that he employs ambiguity, paradox, and self-reference in mundane imagery. We are still left wondering what, exactly, it means, and why, exactly, we respond.

Let us begin with ambiguity. The unconscious participates whenever there is ambiguous input. The phrase *nudisplays* can be heard as "new displays" or "nudist plays," depending entirely upon the predisposition of the listener. It is not a function of the auditory signal but rather of the receiving equipment.

Nudisplays is only ambiguous because it lacks a context. Placed in a sentence, it admits no multiple meanings: "I saw the *nudisplays* in the window of Tiffany's." The surrounding sentence provides a context, and eliminates ambiguity.

There has actually been a good deal of experimental work on perception and context. Psychologist George Miller had subjects listen to a string of words such as *socks, brought, some, wet, who.* Played against a background of static noise, subjects could identify the words correctly only 50 percent of the time. However, when the words were rearranged as *who, brought, some, wet, socks,* identification improved dramatically.

Thus a recognizable context improves perception by invoking a set of anticipations, a set of expectations, which sharpens our focus. Having heard *who brought some* we do not expect to hear a verb, for instance. We expect an adjective, adverb, or noun. We are able to react more quickly, more definitely, to what comes next.

In other cases we fill in gap where something is missing (as a word is missing in this sentence) because we *expect* the word to be there. We may not even be aware that we have filled something in. A certain class of art plays on our desire to fill in, as in Magritte's *The Promenades of Euclid* (1955). Sometimes context provides emotional cues which the stimulus alone does not. In Hitchcock's *Psycho* (1960) this vague image is terrifying. Isolated, it is almost unidentifiable.

Context is thus a powerful tool for sharpening our comprehension of the environment, by allowing us to anticipate what is to come. In *Krapp's Last Tape,* Beckett repeats the word "spool" until all context vanishes, and the naked syllable takes on odd, multiple, conflicting associations. The audience usually laughs. Mark Twain pointed out that almost anything becomes funny if it is repeated often enough, and humor always derives from multiple frames of reference, multiple simultaneous contexts.

Johns employs repetition for other effects. Sometimes he seems to follow Cage's dictum, that if something is boring done once, do it twice; at other times the repeated images are intended to be compared with one another. In either case, the removal of context through repetition is clear. Johns makes the image oscillate between representation and abstraction, between fixed meaning and floating meaning. And in doing so, he allows the unconscious mind freedom to play. This repetition is apparent in his flags, an early image, and in his cross-hatching paintings, his most recent language.

What is the impact of this unconscious freedom? The flag, the familiar image, becomes unfamiliar in a way that re-creates childish awe, the vision of a truly naive observer. We look at it with the blatant curiosity of someone who has never seen a flag before—not because we haven't, but because it is "out of place" in a new setting, and because it is treated in a new way.

The same paradoxical qualities appear in his treatment of numbers. Here is what some children were told about NUMBERS IN COLOR (1958–59):

> You are probably wondering why Jasper Johns painted a picture of numbers. He could have used anything like a flower or something else. He could have made a landscape. But he used numbers. He apparently likes the pattern they can make. He must think them important in their own way. Of course numbers are important to us. We use them to telephone. We use them in the bank. We have to know arithmetic. In the picture, the numbers have nothing to do with telephoning. They have nothing to do with banking or arithmetic. The numbers in the picture are part of a design. They have become something new. They are just shapes and colors repeated and repeated.[33]

Now, one could say more. A critic could point out the competition between elements and overall construction, between the units and the grid in which they are imprisoned;[34] further, the competition between the brush strokes and the numerals defined by the strokes. There is, in nearly all Johns' work, such a competition between structure and imagery, between technique and subject, between the whole and its parts.

But the numbers are, after all, painted abstractions. Here is what Arthur Koestler said about numbers:

> The twentieth-century European regards with justified misgivings the "reduction" of the world around him, of his experiences and emotions, into a set of abstract formulae, deprived of colour, warmth, meaning and value. To the Pythagoreans, on the contrary, the mathematization of experience meant not an impoverishment, but an enrichment. Numbers were sacred to them as the purest of ideas, dis-embodied and ethereal. . . .

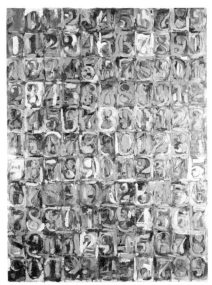

NUMBERS IN COLOR. 1958–59. See Plate 26

0 THROUGH 9. 1961. Charcoal
and pastel on paper, 137.2 x 114.3 cm
(54 x 45"). Private collection

TARGET WITH FOUR FACES. 1955. Encaustic
and collage on canvas with objects,
75.5 x 66 cm (29¾ x 26").
The Museum of Modern Art, New York.
Gift of Mr. and Mrs. Robert Scull

Numbers are eternal while everything else is perishable; they are of the
nature not of matter, but of mind; they permit mental operations of the
most surprising and delightful kind without reference to the coarse
external world of the senses—which is how the divine mind must be
supposed to operate.[35]

Koestler's remarks focus attention on another paradox—the idea of representing what is already an abstraction. The flag, of course, is an abstraction, but most people think of it as a piece of multi-colored cloth. Numbers exist only as intellectual constructs, literally "dis-embodied," and to give them form in a painting is to challenge immediately our ideas of representation and abstraction.

With the targets, Johns goes deeper into ambiguous, psychically rich juxtapositions. In TARGET WITH FOUR FACES, he combines one target and four cut-off faces. There is no obvious link between these two elements, but the viewer is forced to make a connection. Several gifted observers have recorded their attempts.

Leo Steinberg:

Could any meaning be wrung from it? I thought how the human face in this picture seemed desecrated, being brutally thingified—and not in any acceptable spirit of social protest, but gratuitously, at random. At one point, I wanted the picture to give me a sickening suggestion of human sacrifice, of heads pickled or mounted as trophies. Then, I hoped, the whole thing would come to seem hypnotic and repellent, like a primitive sign of power. But when I looked again, all this romance disappeared. These faces—four of the same—were gathered there for no triumph; they were chopped up, cut away just under the eyes, but with no suggestion of cruelty, merely to make them fit into their boxes; and they were stacked on that upper shelf as a standard commodity. . . . I became aware of an uncanny inversion of values. With mindless inhumanity or indifference, the organic and the inorganic had been leveled . . . As if the values that would make a face seem more precious or eloquent had ceased to exist. . . .[36]

David Sylvester:

We speak of a target as a "face"; this is a conventionalized face surmounted by real faces. But are these "real" faces so very much more like faces in reality than the targets are? . . . The plaster faces have no more identity than masked faces. . . . If the target is there to be shot at, maybe the casts are there to be shot at: their absent eyes give them the look of men blindfolded before a firing squad.[37]

Time magazine:

. . . a Johns target, messily painted in red, blue and yellow atop a layer of old newspapers pasted to canvas. Attached to the upper edge of the canvas was a boxlike arrangement containing the lower parts of four faces, done in tinted plaster. The critics have dutifully produced a jargon suitable for such works.[38]

Leo Steinberg, on TARGET WITH PLASTER CASTS:

> Apparently the artist wanted to know (or so he says) whether he could use life-cast fragments of body and remain as indifferent to reading their message as he was to the linage in the newspaper fragments pasted on the canvas below. Could our habit of sentimentalizing the human, even when obviously duplicated in painted plaster—could this pathetic instinct in us be deadened at sight so as to free alternative attitudes? He was tracking a dangerous possibility to its limits; and I think he miscalculated. Not that he failed to make a picture that works; but the attitude of detachment required to make it work on his stated terms is too special, too rare, and too pitilessly matter-of-fact to acquit the work of morbidity.[39]

One cannot read these comments without recognizing the power of ambiguity, its provocative and evocative aspects. The targets have no single meaning, and what we know of the artist's own thinking is no help to us. (Artists are not usually much help; Picasso always said, "It is forbidden to question the pilot.") Steinberg's use of Johns' comments gets him into more trouble than he was in before.

But Steinberg is correct when he says, later, that Johns never again repeats the ruthless juxtaposition of TARGET WITH FOUR FACES. With the exception of UNTITLED (1972), which has a panel of plaster casts of body parts—the artist was consciously worried about these casts being morbidly overpowering, in relation to the whole picture—most of Johns' paintings are calm, almost deferential in their impact on the viewer. Whatever paradoxes they hold are for the viewer to create, and then to worry over.

Max Kozloff:

> . . . the condition of closure, denial, and concealment runs like a *leitmotiv* through this entire gamut of paintings, evoking, as it does, a low-pressure frustration which analysis almost cheapens. After all, the drawer cannot be opened; the canvas will not pry off; nor will the shade roll up, or the envelope unfold. With almost diabolical intent, the artist glues or immolates objects whose everyday function demands some kind of human operation.[40]

Barbara Rose:

> Expectations of cause and effect are not fulfilled. . . . The frustration of expectations created by the disruption of normal cause and effect relationships parallels a similar frustration produced by the knowledge that Johns's apparently useful objects are functionless and inoperative. The newspapers and books can't be read; the piano can't be played; the misshapen cutlery and bent hangers can't be used; the drawers don't open; the traffic lights signal nothing; the canvases can't be painted on. This collection of functional objects deprived of their normal functioning constitutes a depressing catalog of frustrations.[41]

It is important to note that this sense of frustration exists in the mind of the beholder. For example, Johns gives us a canvas with an inset drawer,

Book. 1957. See Plate 17

Disappearance II. 1961. Encaustic and collage on canvas, 101.6 x 101.6 cm (40 x 40″). Private collection

Map. 1961. See Plate 74

implying a space behind the picture plane, but it is we, as observers, who want to open the drawer. And the real reason we want to open the drawer is to prove to ourselves what we already know—that there is nothing behind the canvas plane. He has suggested that there is, as Renaissance perspective suggests, a space behind the picture. But nobody has the urge to step into a Raphael or a Rembrandt; we *look* into it, but remain dutifully outside. Johns has used other means to evoke the same idea of space behind the picture, and this time, we go for it—we buy the idea, at least enough to feel frustrated. There is an uncanny aspect here. One suspects in the end it is the literal quality of Johns' work that accounts for our literal frustration. But beyond this, there is a fundamental conflict between what the eye sees and what the mind knows, a feature of the paintings which is less ambiguous than paradoxical. Those paradoxes are heightened in later work that employs labels.

The device of a label becomes a motif in FALSE START. In its schematic quality, the painting suggests a useful abstraction, a map of some psychic territory of the mind. And indeed, an actual MAP follows two years later, in 1961. Viewing this work, one senses contradiction piled upon contradiction—the use of colors, the naming of states, and the space of the painting employed to evoke, without suggestion, a geographical space of other dimensions.

At the same time, a paradox underlies any map. We are reminded of it by Lewis Carroll:

> "There's another thing we've learned from *your* Nation," said Mein Herr, "map-making. But we've carried it much further than *you*. What do you consider the *largest* map that would be really useful?"
>
> "About six inches to the mile."
>
> "Only *six inches!*" exclaimed Mein Herr. "We very soon got to six *yards* to the mile. Then we tried a *hundred* yards to the mile. And then came the grandest idea of all! We actually made a map of the country, on the scale of *a mile to the mile!*"
>
> "Have you used it much?" I enquired.
>
> "It has never been spread out, yet," said Mein Herr: "the farmers objected: they said it would cover the whole country, and shut out the sunlight! So we now use the country itself, as its own map, and I assure you it does nearly as well."[42]

In other words, the map reminds us that in this case representation is not a substitute so much as a useful tool. A map exists because it has certain advantages over the reality it stands for.[43]

The idea of scale is an important feature here. Kozloff notes:

> . . . scale becomes a very entertaining element. With one movement of the wrist [Johns] can slide from Oklahoma through Kansas into Missouri. And with merely a few strokes, he obliterates most of California, Arizona, Utah, and all of Nevada.[44]

He goes on to observe that the artist is "playing with the notion of measurement, in which the locked-in, diagrammatic 'in scale' dimensions of map images are contrasted with the virtually gratuitous dimensions of painterly gestures, the two being mutually usurped."[45]

Another way to say it is to observe that the artist produces an oscillation between the map (an abstraction representing something) and the painting of the map (an abstraction representing an abstraction) in such a way that multiple ways of looking are simultaneously apparent.

MAP, like FALSE START, also focuses on labels—the verbal abstraction, the linguistic convention. In these paintings, one feels a competition between the language of the painter and spoken or written language. The competition appears literally, as brush strokes obliterate labels and vice versa; and it is felt as we look, and try to make sense of what we see. For just as casts of body parts exert an almost inevitable power, so too do words carry a kind of irreducible impact—and an impact which we are reluctant to give up. (As anthropologist Edmund Carpenter says, "Any word is far more than just a label, a decal, applied or removed at will. It contains meanings & associations & values which help give the thing its identity."[46])

One can think of later paintings, such as OUT THE WINDOW and ZONE, as maps in another sense. We must note a tentative, almost hypothetical quality to these paintings. They suggest other ways of thinking, other possibilities, even as they adopt one way. If they are maps, they chart an uncertain territory; the reality they represent is doubtful and mutable. In fact, there is an attitude toward reality that is reminiscent of the attitude of the Wintu:

> Outside man's experience . . . reality is unbounded, undifferentiated, timeless. Man believes it but does not know it. . . . Within his experience, the reality assumes temporality and limits. As it impinges upon his consciousness he imposes temporary shape upon it. Out of the undifferentiated qualities and essences of the given reality, he individuates and particularizes, impressing himself diffidently and transiently, performing acts of will with circumspection. Matter and relationships, essence, quality are all given. The Wintu actualizes a given design, endowing it with temporality and form through his experience. But he neither creates nor changes; the design remains immutable.[47]

Is this stretching a point about the paintings? I think not; Johns explicitly adopts such an attitude toward reality.

> Time does not pass
> Words pass.
> >—Jasper Johns

> It is believed by most that time passes; in actual fact, it stays where it is. This idea of passing may be called time, but it is an incorrect idea, for since one sees it only as passing, one cannot understand that it stays just where it is.[48]
> >—Dogen, a Zen Master

ZONE. 1962. See Plate 101

SLOW FIELD. 1962. See Plate 104

FIELD PAINTING. 1963–64. See Plate 111

FIELD PAINTING (detail)

Things slip away from the intentions that have located them. Abuses and unexpected uses are found.

— Jasper Johns

"I am thinking," says Zarian, "how nothing is ever solved finally. In every age, from every angle, we are facing the same set of natural phenomena, moonlight, death, religion, laughter, fear. We make idolatrous attempts to enclose them in a conceptual frame. And all the time they change under our very noses."[49]

— Lawrence Durrell

All this implies that a tentative view toward reality is widely held in many disciplines, and indeed it is. It is perfectly apparent in physics. Consider Johns' two paintings—SLOW FIELD (1962) and, particularly, FIELD PAINTING (1963–64). The latter can be described in reference to a color field, a magnetic field, an electric field, a field of view, mirror images, movement. Johns himself thought of an agricultural field, in which a plow turned up a symmetrical furrow of letters. But the letters are hinged, and movable. In earlier paintings, Johns was interested in having the observer move in relation to the paintings; and since the observer could move, why couldn't the elements of the painting move as well? Here they can—a relativistic situation in which the viewer's position and the painting can both change. Further, the participation of the observer in what he sees is directly implied—he can alter the shape of the work, with a touch of his hand.

These are physical ideas, and the relationship of the artist's conception to physics is made more explicit by the magnetic fields of FIELD PAINTING. Walter Thirring said of fields:

Modern theoretical physics . . . has put our thinking about the essence of matter in a different context. It has taken our gaze from the visible—the particles—to the underlying entity, the field. The presence of matter is merely a disturbance of the perfect state of the field at that place; something accidental, one could almost say, merely a "blemish." Accordingly, there are no simple laws describing the forces between elementary particles. . . . Order and symmetry must be sought in the underlying field.[50]

Johns' field paintings may support these abstract associations but are just as concerned with the painter's craft; paintbrushes, solder, and mixing cans litter the field, sticking obstinately to the creation already made, as if they can't be gotten rid of.

This draws our attention to the idea of representation, which has increasingly preoccupied Johns during this period. To measure his involvement, a scale is provided by his tendency to leave behind a literal mark which suggests how the picture was made. From the wooden device in DEVICE CIRCLE (1959) through the handprints in DIVER and LAND'S END, until, finally, the device that scrapes the arc in PERISCOPE (HART CRANE) becomes the artist's arm—we are never allowed to slip into the illusion that the painting is other than a man-made thing, an object in its own right, as well as a representation of something else.

If you want to look at it that way, the devices in these paintings function less to explain than to reinforce doubt. Instinctively, we feel that the devices probably did not make the paintings as they seem to have done; for example, a close look at the scraped arc in PERISCOPE (HART CRANE) leaves us unsure that it was created by the arm we are shown. If the picture wasn't made that way—if the illusion is so obviously an illusion—then we are reminded that the painting itself stands in even more doubtful relationship to whatever it can be said to "represent."

We have already noted a clear additive tendency in the progression of paintings from 1961–64. These images convey a sense of cumulative thought. Looking at the three-paneled RED YELLOW BLUE "flag" of the pictures from the early sixties, one feels that the increasing subtlety of the transformations reflects the logical way that Johns' own thinking proceeds. Kozloff notes that to review Johns' work is not so much to be exposed to a personality as it is to receive an introduction to his way of thought.[51]

The Johnsian system of thought—the attitudes which lead to certain work, and then the perception of limitations which are overcome—has an analogue in physics. Paul Dirac noted that the big advances in physics "usually consist in overcoming a prejudice. We have had a prejudice from time immemorial, something which we have accepted without question, as it seems so obvious. And then the physicist finds that he has to question it, he has to replace his prejudice by something more precise, and leading to some entirely new conception of nature."[52]

And, like physics, the development of Johns' thought has carried him further and further from "common-sense" conceptions of the world. His ideas build upon themselves, working from previously accepted premises toward new problems. Inevitably the later work refers more to his own efforts than it does to present reality.

There is a psychological quality to all this: Rose observes that "most if not all of the work after 1960 must be considered as statements in the past tense." We may feel the intrusion of the artist's own past into his later work, but Rose here seems to be referring to the techniques of painting. "In these works, the record of an action is the trace of a past action. The paintings and prints related to the circular image of *Device* are particularly pessimistic in this respect because they picture the future as only the repetition of the past."[53]

One could look at it that way, and it is true that these paintings have a subterranean uncertainty and even grimness, already noted. But one must recognize that in Johns' method of working—employing a system of thought in a logical manner—the creation of such works is inevitable. A series of logical steps eventually leads to illogic unless the system is broken open, or unless further steps are taken to provide a higher sense of unity.

Consider, for example, the history of mathematics, surely a systematic

PERISCOPE (HART CRANE) (detail). 1963. See Plate 105

DEVICE. 1961–62. See Plate 91

method of thought. As Anatol Rapoport describes the development of numbers,[54] the intrusion of illogical qualities is inevitable. Numbers began with "natural numbers," the numbers we use for counting apples and oranges. Manipulation of these numbers suggested certain abstract actions that could not be carried out: for example, subtracting 8 from 4. Such an action has no meaning in the real world of apples and oranges, but it can be imagined, and once imagined, mathematicians felt obliged to modify their system to make it possible. That is, the equation $a - b = x$ is straightforward when a is greater than b, but if a is less than or equal to b, it is insoluble.

To solve this imaginary equation, the idea of negative numbers and zero had to be introduced. Further inquiry yielded rational integers, rational numbers, real numbers, and complex numbers.

> The new numbers were defined strictly in terms of the old ones, thereby giving logical continuity to the development. . . . At each step toward greater generalization something was gained and something was lost. The gain was enrichment of the theory of numbers. The loss was in intuitive appreciation of the mathematical concepts involved. . . . As mathematicians proceeded to more and more generalization of the number system, intuition suffered more severe insults. This is reflected even in the descriptions by mathematicians themselves: complex numbers, for example, were named "imaginary" numbers, certain functions of real variables were called "pathological," and so forth. . . . Toward the end of the 19th century it seemed that mathematics was on the road to complete emancipation from the illusions of "common sense" and achievement of an ideal science.[55]

This can be said about the history of painting in the nineteenth and twentieth centuries, but it is worth noting that this progression away from common sense characterizes any rigorous body of thought, and that Johns' work—as a logical sequence—seems to have coherence, then to become illogical, then to have coherence, then illogic, and coherence again. But this is a function of the progress of thought, and in that sense Johns' work in the 1960s is very far from pessimistic and certainly does not suggest that the future will be a repetition of the past.

On the other hand, the circularity of the device circle must appeal to Johns. At one time he imagined a number of different "devices" which could leave a mark, a record of activity, on canvas; but he has tended to favor the circle above all others. The circle emphasizes the qualities of paradox. Rapoport notes that "paradoxes arise . . . from failure to pursue a generalization far enough."[56] But at the same time, he recognizes that modern mathematicians now consider paradox inevitable; no system of mathematics can ever be free of it. Johns seems to hold a similar idea.

Paradoxically, it is difficult to define a paradox. Descriptive terms most often employed all apply to Johns' work: self-reference, contradiction, vicious circularity. In its visual forms, paradox is never wholly visual—there is some intellectual aspect invoked.

LIAR. 1961. See Plate 81

> Please Ignore
> This Notice

In order to do it, you must not have done it. Or again:

This sentence is false.

And we have Samuel Butler's famous dictum that "There is only one thing certain, namely that we can have nothing certain; and therefore it is not certain that we can have nothing certain."

Physicists share a delight in paradox. Niels Bohr kept a horseshoe nailed above the door of his country home. A visitor was surprised: surely such a great scientist wasn't superstitious? Bohr said he was not, and that he didn't believe a horseshoe brought luck. "But you know," he added, "they say that it does bring luck even if you don't believe in it!"[57]

Paradox may be truth turned upside down to attract attention; but irony is patent falsehood, its second cousin. Johnsian irony takes many forms—including the most literal "form," the imprint of an iron in the hot wax surface of a painting. This was first seen in PASSAGE (1962), appropriately labeled, where it probably stood as a response to Duchamp's idea to "use a Rembrandt as an ironing board." It re-emerges in WEEPING WOMEN (1975), where its female connotations, breasts and laundresses, are intermingled with the artist's stamp—a kind of ironic handprint—a trace of his work, left on the worked encaustic surface.

PASSAGE. 1962. See Plate 99

Close to irony stands the elusive naiveté, the flat object-ness characteristic of Johns' work. The artist is at some pains to reinforce this: "Well, I'll tell you a secret," he once said, "I don't know anything about art."

But this statement comes from the creator of a painting called LIAR; from a man who has written in his notebook: "Three academic ideas which have been of interest to me are what a teacher of mine [speaking of Cézanne and Cubism] called 'the rotating point of view.'. . . Marcel Duchamp's suggestion 'to reach the Impossibility of sufficient visual memory to transfer from one like object to another the memory imprint'; and Leonardo's idea . . . that the boundary of a body is neither a part of the enclosed body nor a part of the surrounding atmosphere."[58]

These are hardly naive observations. Furthermore, in his work Johns has evolved highly sophisticated concepts about the way perception operates. Compare these two statements:

WEEPING WOMEN. 1975. See Plate 168

> One thing that happens in our experience when we take a point of view toward an object and don't shift our point of view is that one has a heightened sense of the visual nature of the world. But as soon as you move—move your eye, your head, your body—as soon as you approach a work or move away, you have other questions that you can apply to what

THE CRITIC SEES. 1962. Pencil and collage on paper, 26.7 x 36.2 cm (10½ x 14¼").
Collection Mr. and Mrs. Leo Castelli

LIGHT BULB. 1958. See Plate 29

DEVICE. 1962. Oil on canvas with objects, 101.6 x 76.2 cm (40 x 30").
Collection The Baltimore Museum of Art

you're seeing. Not only is that experience important, but the information that this is the case becomes important.

— Jasper Johns

People move. They turn their heads, shift their bodies, walk to the next room, go to the store, or travel around the world. The nature of perception cannot be understood without taking their mobility into account. . . . Perceiving is often most effective during motion. . . . Motion changes the available stimulus information in many ways.[59]

— Ulric Neisser

Neisser is a perceptual psychologist and Johns a practitioner of the applied craft. But if there is no way to presume that the open, literal quality of Johns' work reflects a similar quality of mind, does it tell us anything about his actual perceptions—the way he sees the world?

There is an intriguing speculation here. Johns has said he does not like to wear glasses because he always sees the frames. Most people quickly adjust to spectacles, and soon ignore the frames. That Johns does not suggests that he may lack an ordinary quality of habituation, of accommodation to a constant stimulus.

Accommodation can be shown in a single nerve fiber; with a constant, repetitive stimulus, the fiber fires less often, and finally not at all. Habituation is a cortical analogue; our brains become inattentive to unchanging sensory stimulation. Ordinarily this is a convenience. When we dress in the morning, we briefly feel clothes on our bodies. Soon after, the sensations are extinguished by their constancy.

Taken to a still higher level of abstraction, what we have learned soon becomes unquestioned to us, no longer worthy of conscious attention. How do you turn on the lights in the room? Flick the switch. We do it "without thinking."

Traditionally creativity has been defined as the ability to make connections between previously unconnected things, to "see things a different way." There is now some reason to believe that this ability has a chemical basis, and involves the neurochemical serotonin.[60] Hallucinogens, for example, interfere with normal serotonin metabolism, and such drugs often produce a loss of habituation—ordinary things are freshly seen, as if they were unfamiliar.

There is no reason to believe that all individuals share the same neurochemistry. For Johns, we may speculate that his serotonin-mediated inhibitory mechanisms are more finely adjusted than those of many other people, enabling him to re-create a naive perception—in the best sense of the word.

This is the perception of the child, who sees an object and cannot make sense of it, since sense means, ultimately, adult sense—category formation, linguistic labels, intellectual constructs which eventually become attributes of one thing itself. The competition between fresh seeing and adult instant familiarity appears throughout Johns' work, which is at the same time neither childish nor sophisticated, but both at once.

It is here, finally, that his strength lies. What is truly familiar is not looked at; what is truly new is similarly meaningless. During the nineteenth century, ship's captains liked to fire cannons to startle naive Indians, but the results were always disappointing. The Indians didn't even blink. The loud sound had no meaning to them.

But Johns has always moved along that fine path between what is new and what is known, what is said and what is seen. He sees things with an innocent eye, but re-creates them with the full, overpowering awareness of the adult intellect—and a highly developed artistic skill. By doing so, he evokes the oscillation that exists between a representation and the abstract qualities of that representation. The form his work takes is a peculiarly modern, twentieth-century form. But its power is as old as Paleolithic cave art.

Paleolithic Hand. About 15,000 B.C. Pech-Merle, France

NOTES

1. Lawrence Alloway, "Jasper Johns and Robert Rauschenberg," *American Pop Art,* Collier Books and the Whitney Museum of American Art, New York, 1974, p. 66.

2. Leo Steinberg, "Contemporary Art and the Plight of Its Public" (1962), *Other Criteria: Confrontations with Twentieth-Century Art,* Oxford University Press, New York, 1972, p. 12.

3. *Ibid.,* p. 15.

4. *Discoveries and Opinions of Galileo,* tr. Stillman Drake, Anchor Books, Doubleday, Garden City, N.Y., 1957, p. 238

5. Cited in Jerome Bruner, *On Knowing: Essays for the Left Hand,* Belknap Press, Cambridge, Mass., 1962, p. 66.

6. George Gamow, *Thirty Years that Shook Physics,* Doubleday, Garden City, N.Y., 1966, p. 37.

7. Here is a classic example of the way physics departs from common sense. You can imagine it—or, if you have a light bulb, a razor blade, and a couple of pieces of cardboard, you can verify it for yourself.

   Imagine that light from a source passes through a narrow slit and falls on a surface beyond. What do we see on the surface? The answer is just what you would expect: a bright central area shading off into darkness on both sides.

   Now imagine that the light passes through one slit and strikes a second surface with two slits, and finally reaches a surface beyond. What do we see now? Surprisingly, we find a pattern of vertical light and dark bands, like prison bars. This is how light "arranges itself" when it passes through two slits; it doesn't require expensive equipment to demonstrate, and the fact has been known for a long time.

   How can these bands be explained? It's easy, if you imagine light as a wave phenomenon; just think of the ripple patterns from two pebbles dropped into still water—the outward-spreading concentric circles overlap and interfere with each other. Well, if the two pebbles represent light originating at the two slits, then the final pattern is the result of this outward-spreading interference. That is, at some places the concentric circles will join together to produce a higher wave; at other places the crest of one wave will coincide with the trough of another and cancel out. Such waves of light produce the black bands of cancellation, and the white bands of addition.

   But how do you explain the pattern, if light is a stream of particles, a shotgun blast of pellets? Why should particles passing through two slits distribute themselves in this way? It's no good saying that light is both a particle phenomenon and a wave phenomenon, that sometimes it is more convenient to think of light as particles, and sometimes as waves; that is true enough, but the question remains: How to explain the pattern? In fact, quantum theory can explain interference patterns by saying that *each particle passes through both slits simultaneously.* But that explanation is far from common-sense conceptions of how the world works.

8. Cited in Fritjof Capra, *The Tao of Physics,* Shambhala Publications, Berkeley, Cal., 1975, p. 154.

9. Heisenberg would blanch at this discussion of his work and its origins.

10. In 1964 Heisenberg said (in *Across the Frontiers,* tr. Peter Heath, Harper & Row, New York, 1974, p. 115):

    The best description of these collision phenomena is . . . to speak of the emergence of new particles from the collision energy. . . . We can say that all particles are made of the same fundamental substance, which can be designated energy or matter, or we can put things as follows: the basic substance "energy" becomes "matter" by assuming the form of an elementary particle. In this way the new experiments have taught us that we can combine the two seemingly conflicting statements: "Matter is infinitely divisible" and "There are smallest units of matter" without running into logical difficulties. . . .

11. Sir James Jeans, *The Mysterious Universe,* new rev. ed., Macmillan, New York, 1932, p. 186.

12. John A. Wheeler, "From Relativity to Mutability," in *The Physicist's Conception of Nature,* ed. Jagdish Mehra, Reidel, Dordrecht and Boston, 1973, p. 244.

13. Werner Heisenberg, *Physics and Philosophy,* Harper & Row, New York, 1958, p. 81.

14. An aphorism ascribed to semanticist Alfred Korzybski.

15. Kenneth Clark, *Civilisation,* Harper & Row, New York, 1969, p. 345. He goes on to say: "The incomprehensibility of our new cosmos seems to me, ultimately, to be the reason for the chaos of modern art."

16. Arnold Hauser, *The Social History of Art,* Alfred A. Knopf, New York, 1951, vol. I, p. 334.

17. Guillaume Apollinaire, *Méditations esthétiques—Les Peintres cubistes,* eds. L. C. Breunig and J.-Cl. Chevalier, Hermann, Paris, 1965, pp. 51–52.

18. Anton Ehrenzweig, *The Hidden Order of Art,* University of California Press, Berkeley, Cal., 1967, p. 62.

19. Edmund Carpenter, *Oh, What a Blow That Phantom Gave Me!,* Holt, Rinehart & Winston, New York, 1973, p. 17.

20. A classic example is the use of a watery film-screen to suggest a dream sequence. Utterly arbitrary, its meaning is known only through exposure.

21. Anton Ehrenzweig, *The Psycho-Analysis of Artistic Vision and Hearing,* Routledge and Kegan Paul, London, 1953, pp. 180–81.

22. *Ibid.,* p. 182.

23. A kind of textbook of the psychological meaning of compositions is provided by the films of Akira Kurosawa, particularly the beginning of *Sanjuro* (1962)

and the brilliant, static first half of *High and Low* (1963). Kurosawa conveys character as much by physical orientation of bodies in space as by any other device.

In *To Catch a Thief* (1955), Hitchcock kept Grace Kelly in profile until she finally kissed Cary Grant. "I deliberately photographed [her] ice-cold and I kept cutting to her profile, looking classical, beautiful, and very distant." (Francois Truffaut, with the collaboration of Helen G. Scott, *Hitchcock*, Simon and Schuster, New York, 1967, p. 168.)

24. There is nothing speculative about this sensation. In a particularly interesting comment, Kenneth Clark observes that Leonardo's *Last Supper* has been ineptly restored many times since it was painted. "It is worth insisting on these changes because they prove that the dramatic effect of the *Last Supper* must depend entirely on the position and general movement of the figures, and not on the expression of the heads." (Kenneth Clark, *Leonardo da Vinci*, Penguin, Harmondsworth, England, 1959, p. 92.)

25. The abstraction of folds can be seen in films as well. A striking cut appears in Hitchcock's *Dial M for Murder* (1953), when Grace Kelly's killer hides behind drapes which are first seen as a series of abstract lines, momentarily disorienting the viewer. Another example is the stunning last shot of Kurosawa's *High and Low* (1963).

26. *The Notebooks of Leonardo da Vinci*, ed. Pamela Taylor, New American Library, New York, 1960, p. 28.

27. Georges Clemenceau, *Claude Monet, The Water Lilies*, tr. George Boas, Doubleday, Garden City, N.Y., 1930 (cited in William Seitz, *Claude Monet*, Abrams, New York, 1960, p. 44).

28. The complex intellectual archaeology required to unearth even a portion of the original context of a past artistic creation has been brilliantly dealt with by George Steiner in *After Babel*, Oxford University Press, New York, 1975, *passim*.

29. Cited in Nicholas Wadley, *Cézanne and His Art*, Galahad Books, New York, 1975.

30. See Dean E. Wooldridge, *The Machinery of the Brain*, McGraw-Hill, New York, 1963.

31. Irving S. Bengelsdorf, "Summary of Conference," *Current Research Approaches to Neural Mechanisms of Learning and Memory* (Preliminary Report on a Conference Held at Asilomar Conference Grounds, Pacific Grove, California), U.S. Department of Health, Education, & Welfare, Washington, D.C., Aug. 1975, p. 20.

32. See R. L. Gregory, *The Intelligent Eye*, McGraw-Hill, New York, 1970, p. 30.

33. Charlotte Buel Johnson, "Numbers in Color," *School Arts*, 62, Nov. 1962, p. 35.

34. Amy Goldin, "Patterns, Grids, and Painting," *Artforum*, 14, Sept. 1975, pp. 50–54.

35. Arthur Koestler, *The Sleepwalkers*, Macmillan, New York, 1959, p. 28.

36. Steinberg, *op. cit.*, pp. 12–13.

37. David Sylvester, "Jasper Johns at the Whitechapel," unpublished talk on the BBC *Third Programme*, transmitted Dec. 12, 1964; cited in Max Kozloff, *Jasper Johns*, Abrams, New York, 1969, p. 14.

38. *Time*, 73, May 4, 1959, p. 58.

39. Leo Steinberg, "Jasper Johns: The First Seven Years of His Art" (1962), *Other Criteria: Confrontations with Twentieth-Century Art*, Oxford University Press, New York, 1972, p. 37.

40. Kozloff, *op. cit.*, p. 21.

41. Barbara Rose, "The Graphic Work of Jasper Johns, Part II," *Artforum*, 9, Sept. 1970, p. 66.

42. Lewis Carroll, *Sylvie and Bruno Concluded* (1893), *The Complete Works of Lewis Carroll*, Modern Library, New York, 1936, pp. 616–17.

43. At the same time, we are so accustomed to manipulating symbolic material, we inevitably come to think of symbols as reality itself. (When the first photographs of the earth from space were seen, it was surprising to find that national boundaries were not demarcated, and that different states were not different colors. We knew it, of course, but we had forgotten.)

44. Kozloff, *op. cit.*, p. 28.

45. *Idem.*

46. Carpenter, *op. cit.*, p. 18.

47. Dorothy Lee, "Linguistic Reflection of Wintu Thought" (1944), *Explorations in Communication*, eds. E. Carpenter and M. McLuhan, Beacon Press, Boston, 1960, p. 12.

48. Cited in Capra, *op. cit.*, p. 186. The same sentiment comes also from Austin Dobson:

Time goes, you say? Ah no!
Alas, time stays, we go.

49. Lawrence Durrell, *Prospero's Cell, and Reflections on a Marine Venus*, E.P. Dutton, New York, 1960, p. 105.

50. Walter Thirring (cited in Capra, *op. cit.*, p. 214).

51. Kozloff, *op. cit.*, p. 36.

52. Paul A. M. Dirac, "Development of the Physicist's Conception of Nature " (in Mehra, *op. cit.*, p. 1).

53. Rose, *op. cit.*, p. 71.

54. Anatol Rapoport, "Escape from Paradox," *Scientific American*, 217, July 1967, pp. 50–59.

55. *Ibid*, p. 52.

56. *Idem.*

57. Gamow, *op. cit.*, pp. 57–58.

58. Jasper Johns, quoted in *Sixteen Americans*, ed. Dorothy C. Miller, exhibition catalogue, The Museum of Modern Art, New York, 1959, p. 22.

59. Ulric Neisser, *Cognition and Reality*, W.H. Freeman, San Francisco, 1976, pp. 108–9.

60. See M. A. Geyer and A. J. Mandell, "Euphorohallucinogens—Toward a Behavioral Model," in *Psychopharmacology of Hallucinogens*, eds. R. Willette and R. Stillman, Pergamon Press, Elmsford, N.Y. (in press).

PLATES

1. FLAG. 1955. Encaustic, oil, and collage on fabric, 107.3 x 154 cm (42¼ x 60⅝″). The Museum of Modern Art, New York. Gift of Philip Johnson in honor of Alfred Barr

2

2. FLAG ABOVE WHITE WITH COLLAGE.
1955. Encaustic and collage on canvas,
57.2 x 48.9 cm (22½ x 19¼″).
Collection the artist

3. FIGURE 1. 1955.
Encaustic and collage on canvas,
43.8 x 34.9 cm (17¼ x 13¾″).
Private collection, New York

4. FIGURE 5. 1955.
Encaustic and collage on canvas,
44.5 x 35.6 cm (17½ x 14″).
Collection the artist

5. FIGURE 7. 1955.
Encaustic and collage on canvas,
44.5 x 35.6 cm (17½ x 14″).
Collection Robert H. Halff and
Carl W. Johnson

6. FIGURE 2. 1956.
Encaustic and collage on canvas,
43.2 x 35.6 cm (17 x 14″).
Private collection

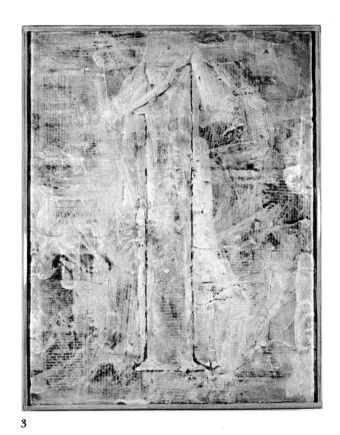

3

4

5

6

7. TARGET WITH PLASTER CASTS. 1955. Encaustic and collage on canvas with objects, 129.5 x 111.8 cm (51 x 44″).
Collection Mr. and Mrs. Leo Castelli

8. WHITE FLAG. 1955. Encaustic and collage on canvas, 198.9 x 306.7 cm (78^{5}/$_{16}$ x 120¾″). Collection the artist

9. FLAG (WITH 64 STARS). 1955. Pencil on paper, 21.5 x 25.7 cm (8½ x 10⅛″). Collection the artist

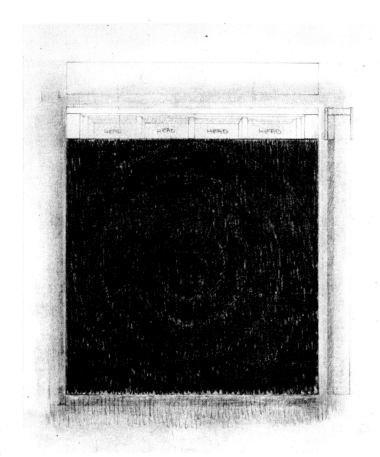

10. TARGET WITH FOUR FACES. 1955.
Pencil on paper,
21.5 x 18.4 cm (8½ x 7¼").
Collection the artist

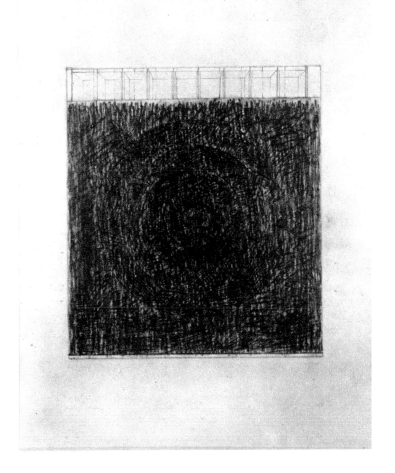

11. TARGET. 1955.
Pencil on paper,
24.2 x 19.1 cm (9½ x 7½").
Collection Mr. and Mrs. Albert Landry,
New York

12. GREEN TARGET. 1955. Encaustic and collage on canvas, 152.4 x 152.4 cm (60 x 60″). The Museum of Modern Art, New York. Richard S. Zeisler Fund, 1958

13. TANGO. 1955. Encaustic and collage on canvas with objects, 109.2 x 139.7 cm (43 x 55″). Collection Mr. and Mrs. Burton Tremaine, Meriden, Conn.

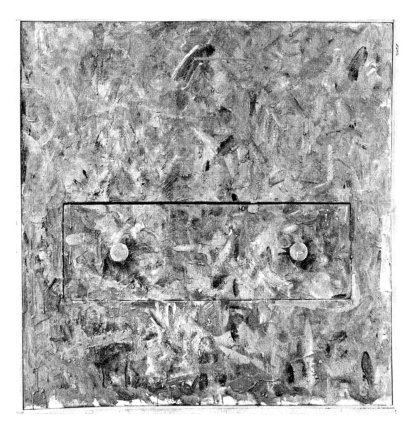

14. DRAWER. 1957. Encaustic on canvas with objects, 77.5 x 77.5 cm
(30½ x 30½″). Brandeis University Art Collection, Rose Art Museum.
Gevirtz-Mnuchin Purchase Fund

15. THE. 1957.
Encaustic on canvas,
61 x 50.8 cm (24 x 20″).
Collection Mildred and Herbert Lee

16. NEWSPAPER. 1957. Encaustic and collage on canvas, 68.6 x 91.4 cm (27 x 36″).
Collection Mildred S. Lee

17. BOOK. 1957. Encaustic with objects, 25.4 x 33 cm (10 x 13″).
Private collection, N.Y.

19. FLAG. 1957. Pencil on paper, 27.6 x 38.9 cm (10⅞ x 15⁵/₁₆″). Collection the artist

18. GRAY ALPHABETS. 1956.
Encaustic and collage on canvas,
167.6 x 124.5 cm (66 x 49″).
Private collection, U.S.A.

20. ALPHABETS. 1957.
Pencil and collage on paper,
36.9 x 26.7 cm (14½ x 10½″).
Collection Robert Rosenblum, New York

21. CANVAS. 1956. Encaustic and collage on canvas with objects, 76.2 x 63.5 cm (30 x 25″).
Collection the artist

22. FLAG ON ORANGE FIELD. 1957.
Encaustic on canvas,
167.6 x 124.5 cm (66 x 49″).
Museum Ludwig, Cologne

23. TARGET. 1958. Oil and collage on canvas, 91.4 x 91.4 cm (36 x 36″). Collection the artist

24. WHITE NUMBERS. 1958.
Encaustic on canvas,
170.2 x 125.8 cm (67 x 49½″).
Museum Ludwig, Cologne

25. Gray Numbers. 1958. Encaustic and collage on canvas, 170.2 x 125.8 cm (67 x 49½").
Collection Kimiko and John Powers, Colorado

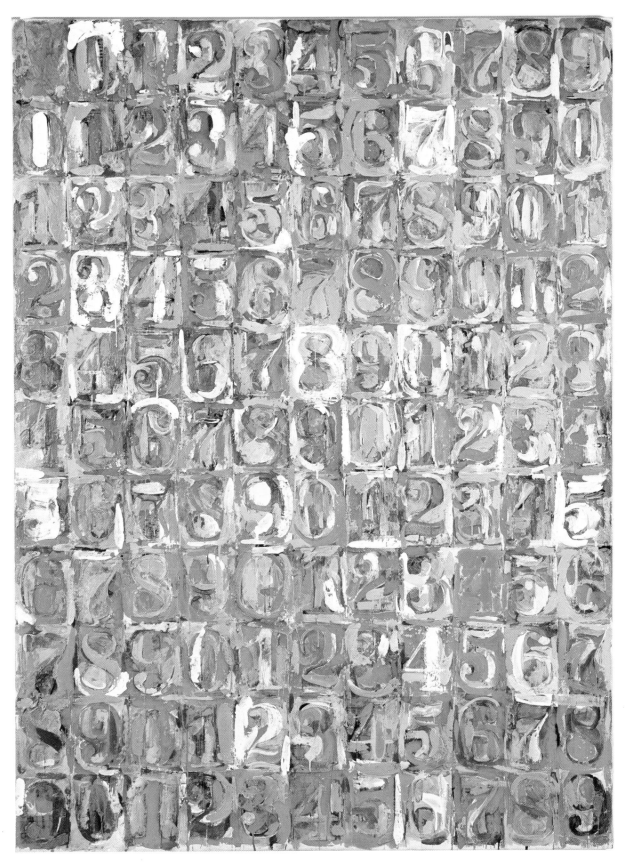

26. NUMBERS IN COLOR. 1958–59. Encaustic and collage on canvas, 170.2 x 125.8 cm (67 x 49½″).
Albright–Knox Art Gallery, Buffalo, N.Y. Gift of Seymour H. Knox

27

28

27. LIGHT BULB I. 1958.
Sculp-metal,
11.5 x 17.1 x 11.5 cm (4½ x 6¾ x 4½″).
Collection Dr. and Mrs. Jack M. Farris

28. LIGHT BULB II. 1958.
Sculp-metal,
7.9 x 20.3 x 12.7 cm (3⅛ x 8 x 5″).
Collection the artist

29. LIGHT BULB. 1958.
Pencil and graphite wash on paper,
16.5 x 22.2 cm (6½ x 8¾″).
Private collection

30. FLASHLIGHT I. 1958.
Sculp-metal over flashlight and wood,
13.3 x 23.2 x 9.8 cm (5¼ x 9⅛ x 3⅞″).
Private collection, New York

31. FLASHLIGHT II. 1958.
Papier-mâché and glass,
7.6 x 22.2 x 10.2 cm (3 x 8¾ x 4″).
Collection Robert Rauschenberg

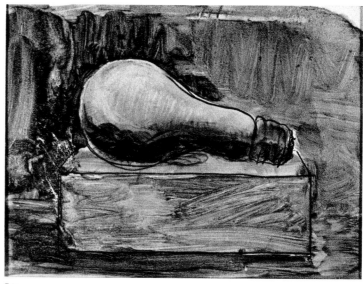

29

30

31

32. FLASHLIGHT III. 1958. Plaster and glass, 13.3 x 9.5 x 20.9 cm (5¼ x 3¾ x 8¼″). Collection the artist

33. ALLEY OOP. 1958.
Oil and collage on cardboard,
58.4 x 45.7 cm (23 x 18″).
Collection Robert Rauschenberg

34. COAT HANGER. 1958.
Crayon on paper,
62.3 x 54.9 cm (24½ x 21⅝").
Collection Mr. and Mrs. William Easton

35. HOOK. 1958.
Crayon on paper,
44.5 x 59 cm (17½ x 23¼").
Private collection, New York

36. GRAY RECTANGLES. 1957. Encaustic on canvas. 152.4 x 152.4 cm (60 x 60"). Collection Mr. and Mrs. Victor W. Ganz

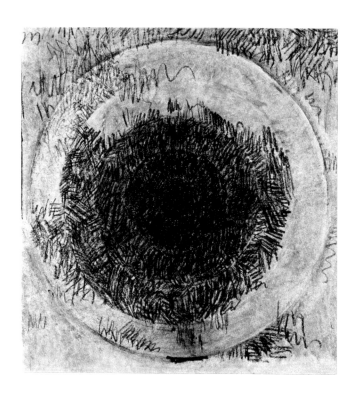

37. BROKEN TARGET. 1958.
Crayon on paper,
39.3 x 38.1 cm (15½ x 15").
Collection Mr. and Mrs. Ben Heller

38. BLACK NUMBERS. 1958.
Crayon on paper,
77.5 x 61 cm (30½ x 24").
Ohara Museum of Art,
Kurashiki, Japan

39. 0–9. 1959. Encaustic and collage on canvas, 51.1 x 88.9 cm (20⅛ x 35″). Collection Ludwig, Aachen

40. THREE FLAGS. 1958. Encaustic on canvas, 78.4 x 115.6 cm (30⅞ x 45½"). Collection Mr. and Mrs. Burton Tremaine, Meriden, Conn.

41. TENNYSON. 1958.
Encaustic and collage on canvas,
186.7 x 122.5 cm (73½ x 48¼").
Des Moines Art Center.
Coffin Fine Arts Trust Fund, 1971

43. THREE FLAGS. 1959. Pencil on paper, 36.9 x 50.8 cm (14½ x 20″).
The Victoria and Albert Museum, London

42. SHADE. 1959.
Encaustic on canvas with objects,
132.1 x 99.1 cm (52 x 39″).
Collection Ludwig, Aachen

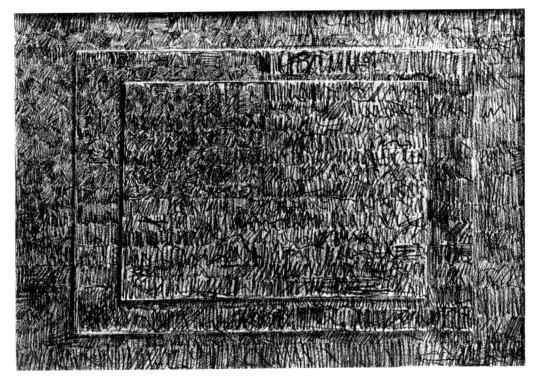

44. THREE FLAGS. 1960. Pencil on paper, 28.5 x 41.9 cm (11¼ x 16½″).
Collection Hannelore B. Schulhof

45. LIGHT BULB. 1960. Painted bronze, 10.8 x 15.2 x 10.2 cm (4¼ x 6 x 4″). One of four casts.
Unlike the other casts, this one has been painted. Collection the artist

46. DEVICE CIRCLE. 1959. Encaustic and collage on canvas with objects, 101.6 x 101.6 cm (40 x 40″).
Collection Mr. and Mrs. Burton Tremaine, Meriden, Conn.

47. Light Bulb. 1960.
Bronze,
10.8 x 15.2 x 10.2 cm (4¼ x 6 x 4″).
One of four casts.
Collection Irving Blum

48. Tennyson. 1958.
Ink on paper,
37.8 x 25.1 cm (14⅞ x 9⅞″).
Collection the artist

49. FLAG. 1960. Sculp-metal and collage on canvas, 31.8 x 48.3 cm (12½ x 19″).
Collection Robert Rauschenberg

50. FLAG. 1960. Bronze, 31.1 x 47.6 cm (12¼ x 18¾″). One of four casts. Collection the artist

51. FALSE START. 1959. Oil on canvas, 170.8 x 137.2 cm (67¼ x 54″). Private collection, New York

52. JUBILEE. 1959. Oil and collage on canvas, 152.4 x 111.8 cm (60 x 44″). Collection David H. Steinmetz

54. TWO FLAGS. 1960. Pencil and graphite wash on paper, 75 x 55.2 cm (29½ x 21¾″). Collection the artist

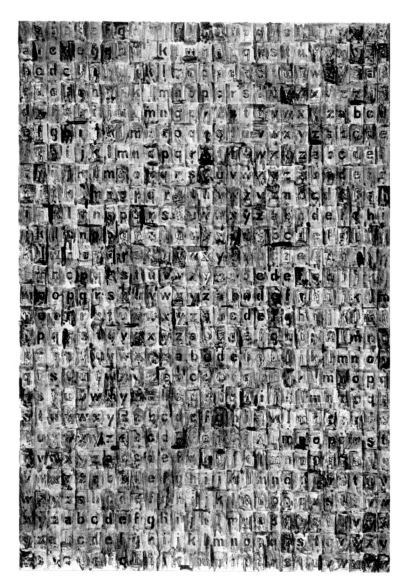

53. GRAY ALPHABETS. 1960. Pencil and graphite wash on paper, 97.5 x 70.8 cm (38⅜ x 27⅞″). Collection Mrs. Leo Castelli, New York

55. TEN NUMBERS. 1960. Charcoal on paper, each 24.1 x 19.1 cm (9½ x 7½″). Collection the artist

56. OUT THE WINDOW. 1959. Encaustic and collage on canvas, 139.7 x 101.6 cm (55 x 40″). Private collection, New York

57. 0 Through 9. 1960. Oil on canvas, 182.9 x 137.2 cm (72 x 54″). Private collection (not in Exhibition)

58. DEVICE CIRCLE. 1960. Pencil on paper, 38.1 x 36.9 cm (15 x 14½"). Collection Mr. Ronald S. Lauder

59. JUBILEE. 1960. Graphite wash on paper, 79.7 x 63.7 cm (31⅜ x 25¹/₁₆"). The Museum of Modern Art, New York. Extended loan from the Lester and Joan Avnet Collection

61. PAINTING WITH TWO BALLS. 1960. Charcoal, pastel, and pencil on paper, 49.6 x 38.7 cm (19½ x 15¼"). Joseph H. Hirshhorn Collection

60. OUT THE WINDOW. 1960. Charcoal and pastel on paper, 87.7 x 72.4 cm (34½ x 28½"). Collection Dr. and Mrs. Bernard Brodsky

62. THE CRITIC SMILES. 1959. Sculp-metal, 4.1 x 19.7 x 3.8 cm (1⅝ x 7¾ x 1½″). Collection the artist

63. PAINTING WITH TWO BALLS. 1960. Encaustic and collage on canvas with objects, 165.1 x 137.2 cm (65 x 54″).
Collection the artist

64. THERMOMETER. 1960. Charcoal and pastel on paper,
56.5 x 41.9 cm (22¼ x 16½"). Collection the artist

65. 0 THROUGH 9. 1960. Charcoal on paper, 73.7 x 58.4 cm
(29 x 23"). Collection the artist

66. HIGHWAY. 1959.
Encaustic and collage on canvas
190.5 x 154.9 cm (75 x 61").
Collection Mrs. Leo Castelli, New York

67. PAINTED BRONZE. 1960. Painted bronze, 14 x 20.3 x 12.1 cm (5½ x 8 x 4¾").
Kunstmuseum Basel, Collection Ludwig

68. PAINTED BRONZE. 1960.
Painted bronze,
34.3 x 20.3 cm diameter (13½ x 8" diameter).
Collection the artist

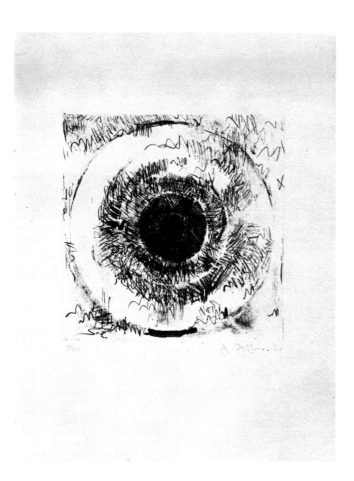

69. TARGET. 1960.
Lithograph,
57.2 x 44.5 cm (22½ x 17½″).
Edition of 30.
Published by Universal Limited
Art Editions

70. FLAG I. 1960.
Lithograph,
55.9 x 76.2 cm (22 x 30″).
Edition of 23.
Published by Universal Limited
Art Editions

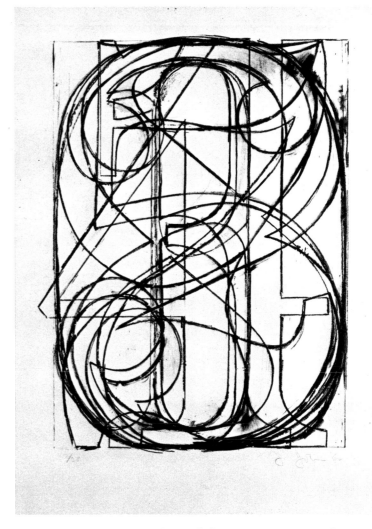

71. COAT HANGER I. 1960. Lithograph, 91.4 x 67.9 cm (36 x 26¾″).
Edition of 35. Published by Universal Limited Art Editions

72. 0 THROUGH 9. 1960. Lithograph, 76.2 x 55.9 cm (30 x 22″).
Edition of 35. Published by Universal Limited Art Editions

73. PAINTING WITH RULER AND "GRAY." 1960. Oil and collage on canvas with objects, 81.3 x 81.3 cm (32 x 32″).
Collection Joseph A. Helman

74. MAP. 1961. Oil on canvas, 198.1 x 312.7 cm (78 x 123⅛"). The Museum of Modern Art, New York. Gift of Mr. and Mrs. Robert C. Scull, 1963

75. 0 THROUGH 9. 1961. Oil on canvas, 137.5 x 105.1 cm (54⅛ x 41⅜″). Hirshhorn Museum and Sculpture Garden, Smithsonian Institution, Washington, D.C.

76. 0 THROUGH 9. 1961. Oil on canvas, 137.2 x 114.3 cm (54 x 45″). Collection Carter Burden, New York

77. 0 THROUGH 9. 1961. Oil on canvas, 137.2 x 114.3 cm (54 x 45″). Collection Mr. and Mrs. S. I. Newhouse, Jr.

78. 0 THROUGH 9. 1961. Oil on canvas, 137.2 x 114.3 cm (54 x 45″). Collection Mr. and Mrs. Frank Titelman, Boca Raton, Fla.

79. BY THE SEA. 1961. Encaustic and collage on canvas, 182.9 x 138.5 cm (72 x 54½"). Private collection, New York

80. No. 1961. Encaustic, collage, and sculp-metal on canvas with objects, 172.7 x 101.6 cm (68 x 40″).
Collection the artist

81. LIAR. 1961. Encaustic, pencil, and sculp-metal on paper,
53.9 x 43.2 cm (21¼ x 17″). Collection Mr. and Mrs. Victor W. Ganz

82. DISAPPEARANCE II. 1962.
Ink on plastic,
45.7 x 45.7 cm (18 x 18″).
Collection The Honorable and
Mrs. Gilbert Hahn, Jr.

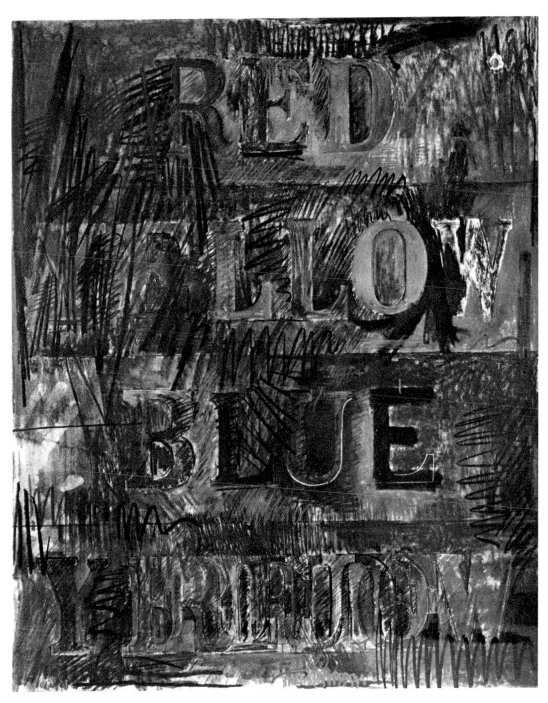

83. FOLLY BEACH. 1962. Charcoal and pastel on paper, 90.2 x 73.7 cm (35½ x 29″).
Anonymous collection

84. IN MEMORY OF MY FEELINGS—FRANK O'HARA. 1961. Oil on canvas with objects, 101.6 x 152.4 cm (40 x 60″).
Collection Dr. and Mrs. Eugene A. Eisner, Scarsdale, N.Y.

85. GOOD TIME CHARLEY. 1961. Encaustic on canvas with objects, 96.5 x 61 cm (38 x 24″). Collection the artist

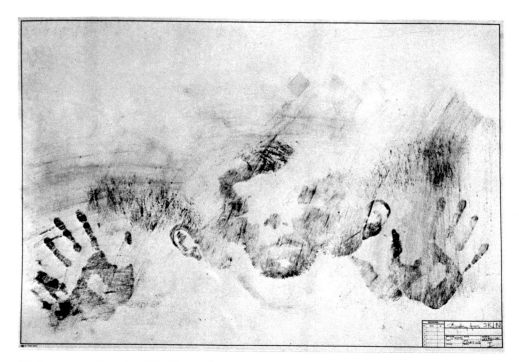

86. STUDY FOR SKIN I. 1962. Charcoal on paper, 55.9 x 86.4 cm (22 x 34″). Collection the artist

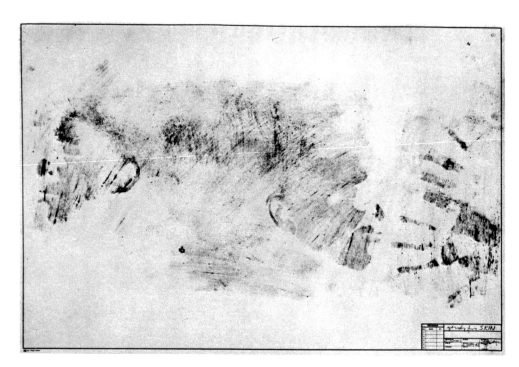

87. STUDY FOR SKIN II. 1962. Charcoal on paper, 55.9 x 86.4 cm (22 x 34″). Collection the artist

88. STUDY FOR SKIN III. 1962. Charcoal on paper, 55.9 x 86.4 cm (22 x 34″). Collection the artist

89. STUDY FOR SKIN IV. 1962. Charcoal on paper, 55.9 x 86.4 cm (22 x 34″). Collection the artist

90. THE CRITIC SEES. 1961. Sculp-metal over plaster with glass, 8.2 x 15.8 x 5.4 cm (3¼ x 6¼ x 2⅛″).
Private collection, New York

91. DEVICE. 1961–62. Oil on canvas with objects,
182.9 x 122.5 cm (72 x 48¼″). Dallas Museum of Fine Arts.
Acquired in honor of Mrs. Eugene McDermott.
Dallas Art Museum League, Mr. and Mrs. George V. Charlton,
Mr. and Mrs. James B. Francis, Dr. and Mrs. Ralph Greenlee, Jr.,
Mr. and Mrs. James H. W. Jacks, Mr. and Mrs. Irvin L. Levy,
Mrs. John W. O'Boyle, Dr. Joanne Stroud

92

93

94

95

92. PAINTING WITH TWO BALLS I. 1962.
Lithograph,
67.3 x 52.1 cm (26½ x 20½″).
Edition of 39.
Published by Universal Limited Art Editions

93. DEVICE. 1962.
Lithograph,
80 x 57.8 cm (31½ x 22¾″).
Edition of 6.
Published by Universal Limited Art Editions

94. FALSE START I. 1962.
Lithograph,
75.6 x 56.5 cm (29¾ x 22¼″).
Edition of 38.
Published by Universal Limited Art Editions

95. FALSE START II. 1962.
Lithograph,
78.7 x 57.2 cm (31 x 22½″).
Edition of 30.
Published by Universal Limited Art Editions

96. 0–9. 1960–63.
Ten lithographs from the portfolio
0–9 (B/C, 1/1, H.C.),
each 52.1 x 40 cm (20½ x 15¾″).
Published by Universal Limited Art Editions.
Collection Mr. and Mrs. Leo Castelli

97. 4 THE NEWS. 1962.
Encaustic and collage on canvas with objects,
165.1 x 127.6 cm (65 x 50¼″).
Private collection, New York

98. FOOL'S HOUSE. 1962.
Oil on canvas with objects,
182.9 x 91.4 cm (72 x 36″).
Collection Mr. Jean Christophe Castelli

99. PASSAGE. 1962. Encaustic and collage on canvas with objects, 137.2 x 101.6 cm (54 x 40″).
Museum Ludwig, Cologne

100. LAND'S END. 1963. Oil on canvas with objects, 170.2 x 121.9 cm (67 x 48").
San Francisco Museum of Art. Gift of Mr. and Mrs. Harry W. Anderson

101. ZONE. 1962. Oil, encaustic, and collage on canvas with objects, 153 x 91.5 cm (60 x 36″). Kunsthaus Zürich

102. OUT THE WINDOW NUMBER 2. 1962. Oil on canvas with objects, 182.9 x 121.9 cm (72 x 48″).
Collection the artist

103. DIVER. 1963.
Charcoal and pastel on paper,
219.7 x 180.3 cm (86½ x 71").
Collection Mr. and Mrs. Victor W. Ganz

104. SLOW FIELD. 1962.
Oil on canvas with objects,
182.9 x 91.4 cm (72 x 36").
Moderna Museet, Stockholm

105. PERISCOPE (HART CRANE). 1963. Oil on canvas, 170.2 x 121.9 cm (67 x 48″). Collection the artist

106. Diver. 1962.
Oil on canvas with objects,
228.6 x 431.8 cm (90 x 170″).
The Albert A. List Family Collection

107. MAP. 1963. Encaustic and collage on canvas, 152.4 x 236.2 cm (60 x 93″). Private collection

108. Untitled. 1963. Charcoal, collage, and paint on paper, 108 x 76.2 cm (42½ x 30″). Collection Mr. and Mrs. Victor W. Ganz

109. Hatteras. 1963. Lithograph, 104.7 x 75 cm (41¼ x 29½″). Edition of 30. Published by Universal Limited Art Editions

110. Skin with O'Hara Poem. 1963–65. Lithograph, 55.9 x 86.4 cm (22 x 34″). Edition of 30. Published by Universal Limited Art Editions

111. FIELD PAINTING. 1963–64.
Oil on canvas, with objects,
182.9 x 93.3 cm (72 x 36¾").
Collection the artist

112. HIGH SCHOOL DAYS. 1964. Sculp-metal over plaster with mirror, 10.8 x 30.5 x 11.5 cm (4¼ x 12 x 4½"). Collection the artist

113. SUBWAY. 1965. Sculp-metal over plaster and wood, 19.4 x 25.1 x 7.6 cm (7⅝ x 9⅞ x 3"). Collection the artist

114. ARRIVE/DEPART. 1963 –64. Oil on canvas, 172.7 x 130.8 cm (68 x 51½″). Private collection, Munich

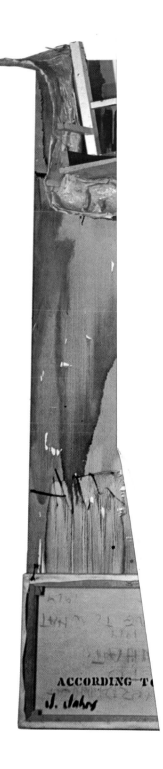

75. According To What. 1964.
l on canvas with objects,
3.5 x 487.7 cm (88 x 192″).
ection Edwin Janss, Thousand Oaks, California

116. SOUVENIR. 1964. Encaustic on canvas with objects,
73 x 53.3 cm (28¾ x 21″). Collection the artist

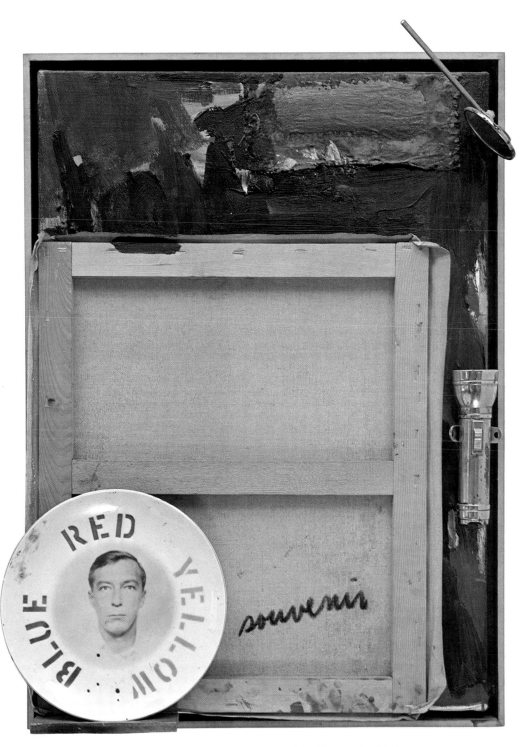

117. SOUVENIR 2. 1964. Oil and collage on canvas with objects, 73 x 53.3 cm (28¾ x 21″). Collection Mr. and Mrs. Victor W. Ganz

118. WATCHMAN. 1964. Oil on canvas with objects, 215.9 x 153 cm (85 x 60¼").
Collection Mr. Hiroshi Teshigahara, Tokyo

119. STUDIO. 1964.
Oil on canvas with objects,
224.8 x 369.6 cm (88½ x 145½").
Whitney Museum of American Art.
Gift of the Friends (and purchase)

120. EDDINGSVILLE. 1965. Oil on canvas with objects, 172.7 x 311.2 cm (68 x 122½"). Museum Ludwig, Cologne

122. ALE CANS. 1964. Lithograph,
57.2 x 44.5 cm (22½ x 17½").
Edition of 31. Published by
Universal Limited Art Editions

121. PINION. 1963–66. Lithograph, 101.6 x 71.1 cm
(40 x 28"). Edition of 36. Published by Universal Limited
Art Editions

123. TWO MAPS I. 1965–66.
Lithograph, 83.8 x 67.3 cm (33 x 26½").
Edition of 30. Published by
Universal Limited Art Editions

124. PASSAGE II. 1966.
Oil on canvas with objects,
151.8 x 158.8 cm (59¾ x 62½").
Harry N. Abrams Family Collection, New York

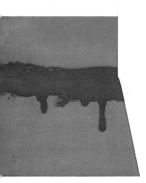

125. Untitled. 1964–65.
Oil on canvas with objects,
82.9 x 426.7 cm (72 x 168").
delijk Museum, Amsterdam

126. WATCHMAN. 1966. Graphite wash, metallic powder, pencil, and pastel on paper, 97.1 x 67.3 cm (38¼ x 26½"). Collection Mr. and Mrs. Victor W. Ganz

127. WATCHMAN. 1967. Lithograph, 91.4 x 61 cm (36 x 24"). Edition of 40. Published by Universal Limited Art Editions

128. STUDIO 2. 1966. Oil on canvas, 177.8 x 317.5 cm (70 x 125″). Collection Mr. and Mrs. Victor W. Ganz

129. HARLEM LIGHT. 1967.
Oil and collage on canvas,
198.1 x 436.9 cm (78 x 172″).
Private collection

130. FLAGS. 1965. Oil on canvas, 182.9 x 121.9 cm (72 x 48″). Collection the artist

131. SCREEN PIECE. 1967. Oil on canvas, 182.9 x 127 cm (72 x 50″). Private collection

132. SCREEN PIECE 2. 1968. Oil on canvas, 182.9 x 127 cm (72 x 50″). Collection Mr. and Mrs. Victor W. Ganz

133. TARGETS. 1967–68. Lithograph, 86.4 x 64.8 cm
(34 x 25½″). Edition of 42. Published by Universal Limited
Art Editions

134. EVIAN. 1968. Graphite, gouache, and pastel on paper,
76.2 x 53.9 cm (30 x 21¼″). Private collection

135. 1ST ETCHINGS. 1967–68. Six etchings from the portfolio 1ST ETCHINGS,
each 63.5 x 50.8 cm (25 x 20″). Edition of 26. Published by Universal Limited Art Editions

136. WALL PIECE. 1968. Oil and collage on canvas, 182.9 x 280 cm (72 x 110¼″). Collection the artist

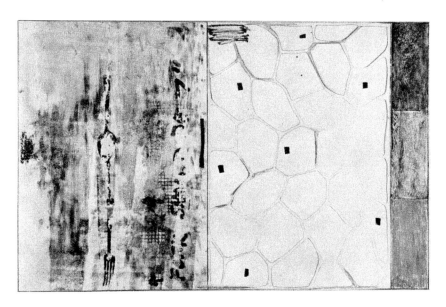

137. WALL PIECE. 1969. Pencil, graphite, pastel, watercolor, and collage on paper, 69.9 x 101.6 cm (27½ x 40″). Collection the artist

138. WALL PIECE. 1969. Ink on plastic, 68.6 x 94 cm (27 x 37″). Collection Mr. and Mrs. Victor W. Ganz

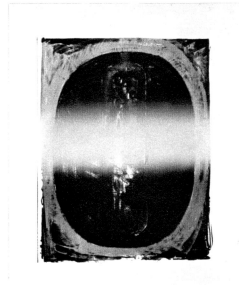

139. FIGURES IN COLOR. 1969.
Ten lithographs, each 98.5 x 78.7 cm (38 x 31″).
Edition of 40. Published by Gemini G.E.L.,
Los Angeles, California

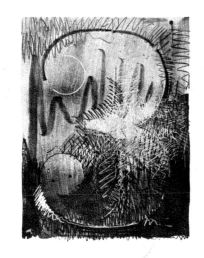

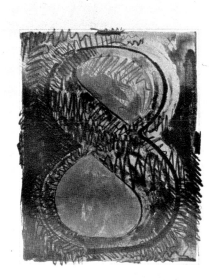

140

140. ENGLISH LIGHT BULB. 1968–70.
Sculp-metal, wire, and polyvinyl chloride,
dimensions variable—length of base 12.4 cm (4⅞″).
Collection Mark Lancaster

141. HIGH SCHOOL DAYS. 1969.
Lead relief with mirror,
58.4 x 43.2 cm (23 x 17″).
Edition of 60. Published by Gemini G.E.L.,
Los Angeles, California

142. BREAD. 1969.
Lead relief with paper and paint,
58.4 x 43.2 cm (23 x 17″).
Edition of 60. Published by Gemini G.E.L.,
Los Angeles, California

143. THE CRITIC SMILES. 1969.
Lead relief with gold and tin,
58.4 x 43.2 cm (23 x 17″).
Edition of 60. Published by Gemini G.E.L.,
Los Angeles, California

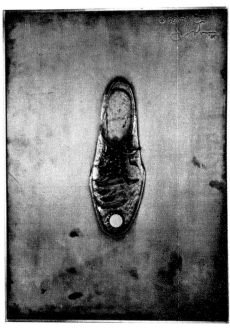

141

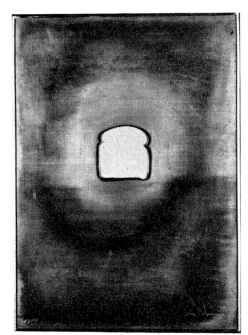

142

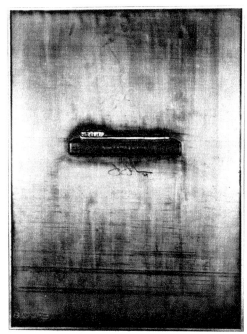

143

144. ZONE. 1969. Graphite, chalk, and gouache on paper, 83.2 x 44 cm (32¾ x 17⁵/₁₆″).
Collection the artist

145. DECOY II. 1971–73. Lithograph, 104.1 x 73.7 cm (41 x 29″).
Edition of 31. Published by Universal Limited Art Editions

146. DECOY. 1971.
Oil on canvas with object,
182.9 x 127 cm (72 x 50″).
Collection Mr. and Mrs. Victor W. Ganz

147. VOICE 2. 1971.
Oil and collage on canvas,
three panels, each 182.9 x 127 cm (72 x 50″).
Kunstmuseum Basel

148. UNTITLED. 1972.
Oil, encaustic, and collage on canvas
with objects,
182.9 x 487.7 cm (72 x 192").
Museum Ludwig, Cologne

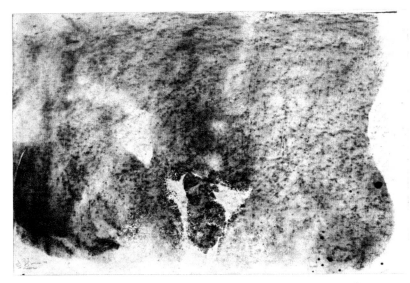

149. Skin I. 1973. Charcoal on paper, 64.8 x 102.2 cm (25½ x 40¼").
Collection the artist

150. Skin II. 1973. Charcoal on paper, 64.8 x 102.2 cm (25½ x 40¼").
Collection the artist

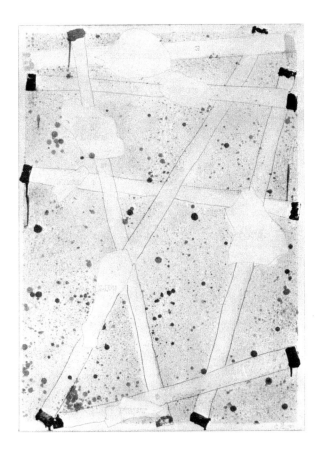

151. Untitled. 1973.
Oil and pencil on paper,
104.7 x 75 cm (41¼ x 29½").
Private collection

152. TWO FLAGS. 1973. Oil and encaustic on canvas, 145.9 x 176.7 cm (57^{7}/$_{16}$ x 69^{9}/$_{16}$"). Collection Jacques Koerfer, Switzerland

153. TARGET. 1974. Encaustic and collage on canvas, 155.5 x 135.5 cm (61¼ x 53¼″).
The Seibu Museum of Art, Tokyo

154

155

156

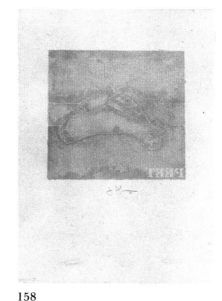

157

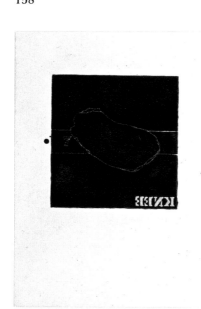

158

159

160

154. FACE. 1974. Lithograph,
78.1 x 57.8 cm (30¾ x 22¾").
Edition of 49. Published by Gemini G.E.L.,
Los Angeles, California

155. HANDFOOTSOCKFLOOR. 1974. Lithograph,
78.1 x 57.8 cm (30¾ x 22¾").
Edition of 48. Published by Gemini G.E.L.,
Los Angeles, California

156. BUTTOCKS. 1974. Lithograph,
78.1 x 57.8 cm (30¾ x 22¾").
Edition of 49. Published by Gemini G.E.L.,
Los Angeles, California

157. TORSO. 1974. Lithograph,
78.1 x 57.8 cm (30¾ x 22¾").
Edition of 50. Published by Gemini G.E.L.,
Los Angeles, California

158. FEET. 1974. Lithograph,
78.1 x 57.8 cm (30¾ x 22¾").
Edition of 47. Published by Gemini G.E.L.,
Los Angeles, California

159. LEG. 1974. Lithograph,
78.1 x 57.8 cm (30¾ x 22¾").
Edition of 50. Published by Gemini G.E.L.,
Los Angeles, California

160. KNEE. 1974. Lithograph,
78.1 x 57.8 cm (30¾ x 22¾").
Edition of 47. Published by Gemini G.E.L.,
Los Angeles, California

161. SCENT. 1973–74. Oil and encaustic on canvas, 182.9 x 320.6 cm (72 x 126¼″). Collection Ludwig, Aachen

162. CORPSE AND MIRROR. 1974. Oil, encaustic, and collage on canvas, 127 x 173 cm (50 x 68⅛″).
Collection Mr. and Mrs. Victor W. Ganz

163. CORPSE AND MIRROR II. 1974–75. Oil on canvas with painted frame, 146.4 x 191.1 cm (57⅝ x 75¼″). Collection the artist

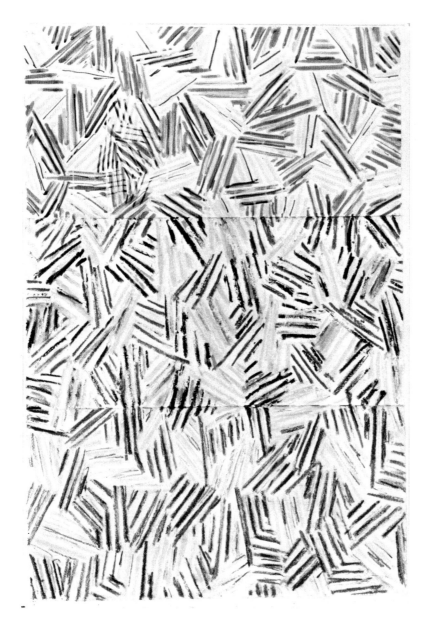

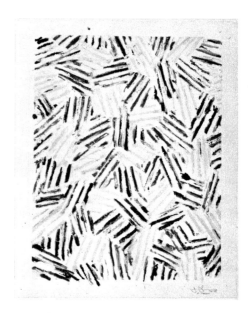

165. UNTITLED. 1974–75. Watercolor and Paintstik on paper, 62.9 x 51.4 cm (24¾ x 20¼″). Collection Janie C. Lee

164. CORPSE. 1974–75. Ink, Paintstik, and pastel on paper, 108 x 72.4 cm (42½ x 28½″). Collection the artist

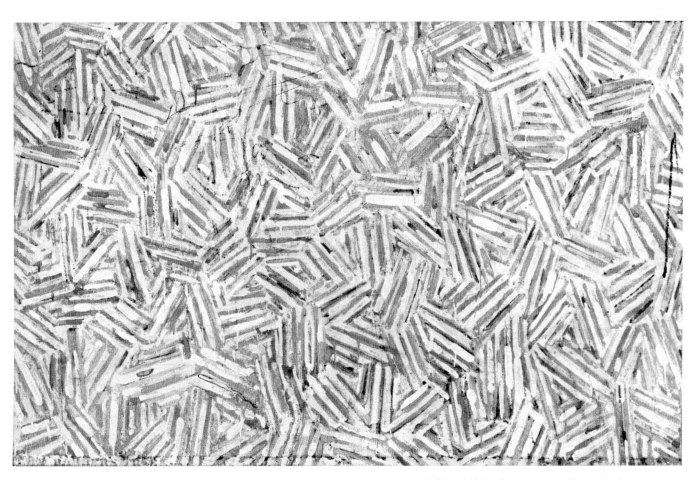

166. THE BARBER'S TREE. 1975. Encaustic and collage on canvas, 87 x 137.8 cm (34¼ x 54¼″). Collection Ludwig, Aachen

167. The Dutch Wives. 1975. Encaustic and collage on canvas, 131.4 x 180.3 cm (51¾ x 71″). Collection the artist

168. WEEPING WOMEN. 1975. Encaustic and collage on canvas, 127 x 259.7 cm (50 x 102¼″). Private collection, New York

169. FOUR PANELS from UNTITLED 1972. (1975)· Lithograph, Four panels, each 104.1 x 81.3 cm
(41 x 32″). Edition of 20. Published by Gemini G.E.L., Los Angeles, California

170. SCENT. 1975 – 76.
Lithograph, linocut, and woodcut,
79.3 x 119.4 cm (31¼ x 47″).
Edition of 42. Published by
Universal Limited Art Editions

171. Corpse and Mirror. 1976.
Silkscreen,
109.2 x 135.2 cm (43 x 53¼″).
Edition of 65. Published by
Simca Print Artists, Inc.

172. END PAPER. 1976. Oil on canvas, 152.4 x 176.6 cm (60 x 69½"). Private collection

Selected Bibliography

Alloway, Lawrence, "The Man Who Liked Cats: The Evolution of Jasper Johns," *Arts Magazine,* vol. 44, no. 1, Sept.–Oct. 1969, pp. 40–43 (a review of Max Kozloff, *Jasper Johns,* Abrams, New York, 1969)

————, "Jasper Johns and Robert Rauschenberg," *American Pop Art* (exhibition catalogue), Collier Books and the Whitney Museum of American Art, New York, 1974, pp. 52–75

Ashbery, John, "Brooms and Prisms," *Art News,* vol. 65, no. 1, March 1966, pp. 58–59, 82–84

Bernstein, Roberta (Introduction), and Robert Littman (Notes), *Jasper Johns' Decoy: The Print and the Painting* (exhibition catalogue), The Emily Lowe Gallery, Hofstra University, Hempstead, N.Y., 1972, unpaginated

————, "Johns and Beckett: Foirades/Fizzles," *The Print Collector's Newsletter,* vol. 7, no. 5 (Nov.–Dec. 1976), pp. 141–45

Cage, John, "Jasper Johns: Stories and Ideas," *Jasper Johns* (exhibition catalogue), The Jewish Museum, New York, 1964, pp. 21–26; reprinted in *Jasper Johns* (exhibition catalogue), Whitechapel Gallery, London, 1964, pp. 26–35; reprinted in John Cage, *A Year from Monday: New Lectures and Writings,* Wesleyan University Press, Middletown, Conn., 1969, pp. 73–84

Calas, Nicolas, and Elena Calas, "Jasper Johns: And/Or," *Icons and Images of the Sixties,* E. P. Dutton & Co., New York, 1971

Castleman, Riva, *Jasper Johns Lithographs* (exhibition catalogue), The Museum of Modern Art, New York, 1970, unpaginated

Coplans, John, "Fragments According To Johns: An Interview with Jasper Johns," *The Print Collector's Newsletter,* vol. 3, no. 2, May–June 1972, pp. 29–32

Field, Richard S., *Jasper Johns: Prints 1960–1970,* The Philadelphia Museum of Art (published in conjunction with Praeger, New York), 1970

————, "Jasper Johns' Flags," *The Print Collector's Newsletter,* vol. 7, no. 3, July–Aug. 1976, pp. 69–77

Fried, Michael, "New York Letter," *Art International,* vol. 7, no. 2, Feb. 25, 1963, pp. 60–62

Geldzahler, Henry, "Numbers in Time: Two American Paintings," *The Metropolitan Museum of Art Bulletin,* vol. 23, no. 8, April 1965, pp. 295–99

Greenberg, Clement, "After Abstract Expressionism," *Art International,* vol. 6, no. 8, Oct. 25, 1962, pp. 24–32; revised and reprinted in Henry Geldzahler, *New York Painting and Sculpture: 1940–1970,* E. P. Dutton & Co., in association with The Metropolitan Museum of Art, New York, 1969, pp. 360–71

Heller, Ben, "Jasper Johns," *School of New York: Some Younger Artists,* ed. B. H. Friedman, Grove Press, New York, 1959, pp. 30–35

Hess, Thomas B., "On the Scent of Jasper Johns," *New York Magazine,* vol. 9, no. 6, Feb. 9, 1976, pp. 65–67

Higginson, Peter, "Jasper's Non-Dilemma: A Wittgensteinian Approach," *New Lugano Review,* no. 10, 1976, pp. 53–60

Hopkins, Henry, "Jasper Johns: Figures 0 to 9" (brochure), Gemini G.E.L., Los Angeles, 1968

Hopps, Walter, "An Interview with Jasper Johns," *Artforum,* vol. 3, no. 6, March 1965, pp. 32–36

————, "Jasper Johns: Fragments—According To What" (brochure), Gemini G.E.L., Los Angeles, 1971

Huber, Carlo, "Jasper Johns: Die Graphik," *Jasper Johns Graphik,* ed. Carlo Huber, Kornfeld und Klipstein, Bern, 1970

Johns, Jasper [statement], *Sixteen Americans* (exhibition catalogue), ed. Dorothy C. Miller, The Museum of Modern Art, New York, 1959, pp. 22–27; reprinted in Barbara Rose (ed.), *Readings in American Art Since 1900: A Documentary Survey,* Praeger, New York, 1968, pp. 165–66

————, "Duchamp," *Scrap,* vol. 2, Dec. 23, 1960, p. 4 (a review of *The Bride Stripped Bare By Her Bachelors, Even,* a typographic version by Richard Hamilton of Marcel Duchamp's *Green Box,* translated by George Heard Hamilton, *The Documents of Modern Art,* no. 14, Wittenborn, New York, 1960)

————, "Sketchbook Notes," *Art and Literature* (Lausanne), vol. 4, Spring 1965, pp. 185–92; reprinted in John Russell and Suzi Gablik, *Pop Art Redefined,* Thames and Hudson, London, 1969, pp. 84–85

————, "Marcel Duchamp (1887–1968): An Appreciation," *Artforum,* vol. 7, no. 3 (Nov. 1968), p. 6; reprinted in Anne d'Harnoncourt and Kynaston McShine (eds.), *Marcel Duchamp,* The Museum of Modern Art, New York, 1973, pp. 203–4

————, "Sketchbook Notes," *Juillard,* ed. [and publ.]

Trevor Winkfield, Winter 1968–69, pp. 25–27

———, "Sketchbook Notes," *Art Now: New York,* vol. 1, no. 4, April 1969

———, "Thoughts on Duchamp," *Art in America,* vol. 57, no. 4, July–Aug. 1969, p. 31

Johnson, Ellen H., "Jim Dine and Jasper Johns: Art about Art," *Art and Literature* (Lausanne), vol. 6, Autumn 1965, pp. 128–40; reprinted in Ellen H. Johnson, *Modern Art and the Object,* Harper and Row, New York, 1976, pp. 171–76

Kaplan, Patricia, "On Jasper Johns' *According To What,*" *Art Journal,* vol. 35, no. 3, Spring 1976, pp. 247–50

Kozloff, Max, "Johns and Duchamp," *Art International,* vol. 3, no. 2, March 1964, pp. 42–45

———, *Jasper Johns,* Abrams, New York, 1969

———, *Jasper Johns,* Abrams/Meridian Modern Artists, New York, 1974

Krauss, Rosalind, "Jasper Johns," *Lugano Review II,* vol. 1, no. 2, 1965, pp. 84–114

———, "Jasper Johns: The Functions of Irony," *October,* vol. 2, Summer 1976, pp. 91–99

Masheck, Joseph, "Sit-in on Johns," *Studio International,* vol. 178, no. 916, pp. 193–95 (a review of Max Kozloff, *Jasper Johns,* Abrams, New York, 1969)

———, "Jasper Johns Returns," *Art in America,* vol. 64, no. 2, March–April 1976, pp. 65–67

Michelson, Annette, "The Imaginary Object: Recent Prints by Jasper Johns," *Artist's Proof,* vol. 8, 1968, pp. 44–49

Perrone, Jeff, "Jasper Johns's New Paintings," *Artforum,* vol. 14, no. 8, Apr. 1976, pp. 48–51

Porter, Fairfield, "The Education of Jasper Johns," *Art News,* vol. 62, no. 10, Feb. 1964, pp. 44, 61–62

Raynor, Vivian, "Conversation with Jasper Johns," *Art News,* vol. 72, no. 3, March 1973, pp. 20–22

Rose, Barbara, "The Graphic Work of Jasper Johns: Part I," *Artforum,* vol. 8, no. 7, March 1970, pp. 39–45

———, "The Graphic Work of Jasper Johns: Part II," *Artforum,* vol. 8, no. 9, Sept. 1970, pp. 65–74

———, "Decoys and Doubles: Jasper Johns and the Modernist Mind," *Arts Magazine,* vol. 50, no. 9, May 1976, pp. 68–73

Rosenberg, Harold, "Jasper Johns: Things the Mind Already Knows." *Vogue,* vol. 143, no. 3, Feb. 1, 1964, pp. 175–77, 201–3; reprinted in Harold Rosenberg, *The Anxious Object: Art Today and Its Audience,* Collier Books, New York, 1973, pp. 176–84

Rosenblum, Robert, "Jasper Johns," *Art International,* vol. 4, no. 7, Sept. 1960, pp. 74–77

———, "Les Oeuvres Récentes de Jasper Johns," *XXe Siècle,* vol. 24, no. 18, Feb. 1962, supplement, unpaginated

———, [Preface to Portfolio 0–9] Universal Limited Art Editions, West Islip, N.Y., 1963

Rubin, William, "Younger American Painters," *Art International,* vol. 4, no. 1, 1960, pp. 24–31

Russell, John, "Jasper Johns and the Readymade Image," in *The Meanings of Modern Art,* vol. 11, The Museum of Modern Art, New York, 1975, pp. 15–23

Shapiro, David, "Imago Mundi," *Art News,* vol. 70, no. 6, Oct. 1971, pp. 40–41, 66–68

Solomon, Alan R., "Jasper Johns," *Jasper Johns* (exhibition catalogue), The Jewish Museum, New York, 1964, pp. 5–19; reprinted in *Jasper Johns* (exhibition catalogue), Whitechapel Gallery, London, 1964, pp. 4–25

———, "Jasper Johns: Lead Reliefs" (brochure), Gemini G.E.L., Los Angeles, 1969

Steinberg, Leo, "Contemporary Art and the Plight of Its Public," *Harper's Magazine,* vol. 224, no. 1342, March 1962, pp. 31–39; reprinted in Leo Steinberg, *Other Criteria: Confrontations with Twentieth-Century Art,* Oxford University Press, New York, 1972

———, "Jasper Johns," *Metro,* nos. 4/5, May 1962; enlarged and revised for *Jasper Johns,* Wittenborn, New York, 1963; revised and expanded as "Jasper Johns: The First Seven Years of His Art," in *Other Criteria: Confrontations with Twentieth-Century Art,* Oxford University Press, New York, 1972

Swenson, G. R., "What is Pop Art? Part II [Interview with Jasper Johns, *i.a.*]," *Art News,* vol. 62, no. 10, Feb. 1964, pp. 40–43, 62–67; reprinted in John Russell and Suzi Gablik, *Pop Art Redefined,* Thames and Hudson, London, 1969, pp. 82–83

Sylvester, David, "Interview," *Jasper Johns Drawings* (catalogue of the exhibition organized by the Arts Council of Great Britain), 1974, pp. 7–19

Tillim, Sidney, "Ten Years of Jasper Johns," *Arts Magazine,* vol. 38, no. 7, April 1964, pp. 22–26

Young, Joseph E., "Jasper Johns: An Appraisal," *Art International,* vol. 13, no. 7, Sept. 1969, pp. 50–56

Alphabetical List of Illustrated Works by Jasper Johns

The works are identified as (p) painting; (s) sculpture; (d) drawing; (pr) print

WATCHMAN (1964) (p), Pl. 118; p. 51, below

WATCHMAN (1966) (d), Pl. 126

WATCHMAN (1967) (pr), Pl. 127

WEEPING WOMEN (1975) (p), Pl. 168; p. 95, below

WHITE FLAG (1955) (p), Pl. 8

WHITE NUMBERS (1958) (p), Pl. 24

WHITE TARGET (1957) (p), p. 21, above

0 [Zero], see FIGURE 0; also 0–9, FIGURES IN COLOR, TEN NUMBERS

0–9 (1959) (p), Pl. 39

0–9 (1960–63) (pr), Pl. 96

0 THROUGH 9 (1960) (p), Pl. 57

0 THROUGH 9 (1960) (d), Pl. 65

0 THROUGH 9 (1960) (pr), Pl. 72

0 THROUGH 9 (1961) (p), Pls. 75, 76, 77, 78

0 THROUGH 9 (1961) (d), p. 88, above

0 Through 9, see also 1st [First] ETCHINGS

ZONE (1962) (p), Pl. 101; p. 50, above

ZONE (1969) (d), Pl. 144

Changes in caption and Checklist entry for the following pictures should be noted:

Plate 61 (Checklist 66), Hirshhorn Museum and Sculpture Garden, Smithsonian Institution, Washington, D.C.

Plate 73 (Checklist 53), Collection Gustaf Douglas, Stockholm

Plate 100, The San Francisco Museum of Modern Art, San Francisco, Cal.

Photographic Credits

The author and publisher wish to thank the owners and custodians for permitting the reproduction of the works of art in their collections. Photographs have been supplied by the following, whose courtesy is gratefully acknowledged: Leo Castelli Gallery, New York; Gemini G.E.L., Los Angeles; Universal Limited Art Editions, West, Islip, N.Y.; as well as by the photographers and photographic services listed below. Alinari—Art Reference Bureau (Florence), Pages 52, above; 82, above, middle; Allison, David, Pl. 12; Burckhardt, Rudolph, Pls. 4, 14, 15, 16, 17, 23, 24, 27, 29, 30, 34, 35, 37, 42, 43, 44, 47, 48, 49, 50, 53, 54, 58, 59, 60, 61, 66, 76, 77, 78, 81, 96, 99, 100, 103, 113, 123, 126, 127, 130, 131, 132, 134, 136, 137. Pages 17; 18, above, below; 19; 26, below; 28; 29; 30, above, below; 31, below; 33, below; 35, above; 37, below; 39, above; 42, above; 43, below; 45, below; 47, above; 48, above; 49, above, below; 52, below; 53, left; 54, middle, below; 56, below; 77, above; 80, above; 85; 92, above, middle; 93, below; 95, above, middle; 96, middle; Clements, Geoffrey, Pl. 119. Page 21, above; 37, above; Cornachio, Ed, Pls. 139B, 139E, 139G, 139J; Darmstaedter, Frank, Page 36; Gabinetto Fotografico Nazionale (Florence), Page 81, below; Hinz (Basel), Pl. 67; Jones, Bruce C., Pls. 20, 39, 153; Katz, Michael, Page 87; Lubliner, Malcolm, Pls. 139A, 139H, 141, 142, 143, 157, 159; Pages 13, above; 86, above; Mates, Robert, and Donlon, Mary, Pl. 172; McDarrah, Fred W., Page 40; Pollitzer, Eric, Pls. 2, 6, 10, 11, 28, 31, 45, 62, 64, 68, 82, 83, 84, 85, 90, 97, 98, 108, 112, 116, 117, 120, 124, 139, 140, 144, 146, 149, 150, 151, 152, 161, 163, 164, 166, 167, 171; Pages 43, above; 56, above; 58; 59, below; 60; 62, above, below; 95, below; 96, above, below; Rule, Lloyd W., Pl. 25; Shunk, Harry, Pl. 9; Shunk-Kender, Pls. 19, 55 A-J, 65, 86, 87, 88, 89; Page 13, above; 35, middle; 82, bottom; Sonnabend Gallery (New York), Pl. 3; Szaszfai, Joseph, Page 79; Thomas, Frank J., Pages 27, above; 80, middle; Thomson, Jann & John, Pl. 5; Page 31, middle; Universal City Studios, Inc. (with permission of Universal City Studios, Inc., and Alfred Hitchcock), Page 86, below; Varon, Malcolm, Pl. 74.

Checklist of the Exhibition

1. FLAG. 1955. Encaustic, oil, and collage on fabric, 107.3 x 154 cm (42¼ x 60⅝"). The Museum of Modern Art, New York. Gift of Philip Johnson in honor of Alfred Barr

2. TARGET WITH PLASTER CASTS. 1955. Encaustic and collage on canvas with objects, 129.5 x 111.8 cm (51 x 44"). Collection Mr. and Mrs. Leo Castelli

3. WHITE FLAG. 1955. Encaustic and collage on canvas, 198.9 x 306.7 cm (78⁵⁄₁₆ x 120¾"). Collection the artist

4. FLAG ABOVE WHITE WITH COLLAGE. 1955. Encaustic and collage on canvas, 57.2 x 48.9 cm (22½ x 19¼"). Collection the artist

5. FIGURE 1. 1955. Encaustic and collage on canvas, 43.8 x 34.9 cm (17¼ x 13¾"). Private collection, New York

6. FIGURE 2. 1956. Encaustic and collage on canvas, 43.2 x 35.6 cm (17 x 14"). Private collection

7. FIGURE 5. 1955. Encaustic and collage on canvas, 44.5 x 35.6 cm (17½ x 14"). Collection the artist

8. FIGURE 7. 1955. Encaustic and collage on canvas, 44.5 x 35.6 cm (17½ x 14"). Collection Robert H. Halff and Carl W. Johnson

9. GREEN TARGET. 1955. Encaustic and collage on canvas, 152.4 x 152.4 cm (60 x 60"). The Museum of Modern Art, New York. Richard S. Zeisler Fund, 1958

10. TANGO. 1955. Encaustic and collage on canvas with objects, 109.2 x 139.7 cm (43 x 55"). Collection Mr. and Mrs. Burton Tremaine, Meriden, Conn.

11. FLAG (with 64 stars). 1955. Pencil on paper, 21.5 x 25.7 cm (8½ x 10⅛"). Collection the artist

12. TARGET WITH FOUR FACES. 1955. Pencil on paper, 21.5 x 18.4 cm (8½ x 7¼"). Collection the artist

13. TARGET. 1955. Pencil on paper, 24.2 x 19.1 cm (9½ x 7½"). Collection Mr. and Mrs. Albert Landry, New York

14. GRAY ALPHABETS. 1956. Encaustic and collage on canvas, 167.6 x 124.5 cm (66 x 49"). Private collection, U.S.A.

15. CANVAS. 1956. Encaustic and collage on canvas with objects, 76.2 x 63.5 cm (30 x 25"). Collection the artist

16. FLAG ON ORANGE FIELD. 1957. Encaustic on canvas, 167.6 x 124.5 cm (66 x 49"). Museum Ludwig, Cologne

17. GRAY RECTANGLES. 1957. Encaustic on canvas, 152.4 x 152.4 cm (60 x 60"). Collection Mr. and Mrs. Victor W. Ganz

18. DRAWER. 1957. Encaustic on canvas with objects, 77.5 x 77.5 cm (30½ x 30½"). Brandeis University Art Collection, Rose Art Museum. Gevirtz-Mnuchin Purchase Fund

19. NEWSPAPER. 1957. Encaustic and collage on canvas, 68.6 x 91.4 cm (27 x 36"). Collection Mildred S. Lee

20. THE. 1957. Encaustic on canvas, 61 x 50.8 cm (24 x 20"). Collection Mildred and Herbert Lee

21. BOOK. 1957. Encaustic with objects, 25.4 x 33 cm (10 x 13"). Private collection, N.Y.

22. FLAG. 1957. Pencil on paper, 27.6 x 38.9 cm (10⅞ x 15⁵⁄₁₆"). Collection the artist

23. ALPHABETS. 1957. Pencil and collage on paper, 36.9 x 26.7 cm (14½ x 10½"). Collection Robert Rosenblum, New York

24. GRAY NUMBERS. 1958. Encaustic and collage on canvas, 170.2 x 125.8 cm (67 x 49½"). Collection Kimiko and John Powers, Colorado

25. WHITE NUMBERS. 1958. Encaustic on canvas, 170.2 x 125.8 cm (67 x 49½"). Museum Ludwig, Cologne

26. NUMBERS IN COLOR. 1958–59. Encaustic and collage on canvas, 170.2 x 125.8 cm (67 x 49½"). Albright–Knox Art Gallery, Buffalo, N.Y. Gift of Seymour H. Knox

27. TARGET. 1958. Oil and collage on canvas, 91.4 x 91.4 cm (36 x 36"). Collection the artist

28. THREE FLAGS. 1958. Encaustic on canvas, 78.4 x 115.6 cm (30⅞ x 45½"). Collection Mr. and Mrs. Burton Tremaine, Meriden, Conn.

29. TENNYSON. 1958. Encaustic and collage on canvas, 186.7 x 122.5 cm (73½ x 48¼"). Des Moines Art Center. Coffin Fine Arts Trust Fund, 1971

30. ALLEY OOP. 1958. Oil and collage on cardboard, 58.4 x 45.7 cm (23 x 18"). Collection Robert Rauschenberg

31. LIGHT BULB I. 1958. Sculp-metal, 11.5 x 17.1 x 11.5 cm (4½ x 6¾ x 4½"). Collection Dr. and Mrs. Jack M. Farris

32. LIGHT BULB II. 1958. Sculp-metal, 7.9 x 20.3 x 12.7 cm (3⅛ x 8 x 5"). Collection the artist

33. FLASHLIGHT I. 1958. Sculp-metal over flashlight and wood, 13.3 x 23.2 x 9.8 cm (5¼ x 9⅛ x 3⅞"). Private collection, New York

34. FLASHLIGHT II. 1958. Papier-mâché and glass, 7.6 x 22.2 x 10.2 cm (3 x 8¾ x 4"). Collection Robert Rauschenberg

35. FLASHLIGHT III. 1958. Plaster and glass, 13.3 x 9.5 x 20.9 cm (5¼ x 3¾ x 8¼"). Collection the artist

36. LIGHT BULB. 1958. Pencil and graphite wash on paper, 16.5 x 22.2 cm (6½ x 8¾"). Private collection

37. COAT HANGER. 1958. Crayon on paper, 62.3 x 54.9 cm (24½ x 21⅝"). Collection Mr. and Mrs. William Easton

38. HOOK. 1958. Crayon on paper, 44.5 x 59 cm (17½ x 23¼"). Private collection, New York

39. BROKEN TARGET. 1958. Crayon on paper, 39.3 x 38.1 cm (15½ x 15"). Collection Mr. and Mrs. Ben Heller

40. BLACK NUMBERS. 1958. Crayon on paper, 77.5 x 61 cm (30½ x 24"). Ohara Museum of Art

41. TENNYSON. 1958. Ink on paper, 37.8 x 25.1 cm (14⅞ x 9⅞"). Collection the artist

42. 0–9. 1959. Encaustic and collage on canvas, 51.1 x 88.9 cm (20⅛ x 35"). Collection Ludwig, Aachen

43. DEVICE CIRCLE. 1959. Encaustic and collage on canvas with objects, 101.6 x 101.6 cm (40 x 40"). Collection Mr. and Mrs. Burton Tremaine, Meriden, Conn.

44. FALSE START. 1959. Oil on canvas, 170.8 x 137.2 cm (67¼ x 54"). Private collection, New York

45. JUBILEE. 1959. Oil and collage on canvas, 152.4 x 111.8 cm (60 x 44"). Collection David H. Steinmetz

46. OUT THE WINDOW. 1959. Encaustic and collage on canvas, 139.7 x 101.6 cm (55 x 40"). Private collection, New York

47. SHADE. 1959. Encaustic on canvas with objects, 132.1 x 99.1 cm (52 x 39"). Collection Ludwig, Aachen

48. HIGHWAY. 1959. Encaustic and collage on canvas, 190.5 x 154.9 cm (75 x 61"). Collection Mrs. Leo Castelli, New York

49. THE CRITIC SMILES. 1959. Sculp-metal, 4.1 x 19.7 x 3.8 cm (1⅝ x 7¾ x 1½"). Collection the artist

50. THREE FLAGS. 1959. Pencil on paper, 36.9 x 50.8 cm (14½ x 20"). The Victoria and Albert Museum, London

51. PAINTING WITH TWO BALLS. 1960. Encaustic and collage on canvas with objects, 165.1 x 137.2 cm (65 x 54"). Collection the artist

52. FLAG. 1960. Sculp-metal and collage on canvas, 31.8 x 48.3 cm (12½ x 19"). Collection Robert Rauschenberg

53. PAINTING WITH RULER AND "GRAY." 1960. Oil and collage on canvas with objects, 81.3 x 81.3 cm (32 x 32"). Collection Joseph A. Helman

54. PAINTED BRONZE. 1960. Painted bronze, 14 x 20.3 x 12.1 cm (5½ x 8 x 4¾"). Kunstmuseum Basel, Collection Ludwig

55. PAINTED BRONZE. 1960. Painted bronze, 34.3 x 20.3 (diameter) cm (13½ x 8 (diameter)"). Collection the artist

56. LIGHT BULB. 1960. Bronze, 10.8 x 15.2 x 10.2 cm (4¼ x 6 x 4"). One of four casts. Collection Irving Blum

57. LIGHT BULB. 1960. Painted bronze, 10.8 x 15.2 x 10.2 cm (4¼ x 6 x 4"). One of four casts. Unlike the other casts, this one has been painted. Collection the artist

58. FLAG. 1960. Bronze, 31.1 x 47.6 cm (12¼ x 18¾"). One of four casts. Collection the artist

59. THREE FLAGS. 1960. Pencil on paper, 28.5 x 41.9 cm (11¼ x 16½"). Collection Hannelore B. Schulhof

60. GRAY ALPHABETS. 1960. Pencil and graphite wash on paper, 97.5 x 70.8 cm (38⅜ x 27⅞"). Collection Mrs. Leo Castelli, New York

61. TWO FLAGS. 1960. Pencil and graphite wash on paper, 75 x 55.2 cm (29½ x 21¾"). Collection the artist

62 A. FIGURE 0 (from TEN NUMBERS). 1960. Charcoal on paper, 24.1 x 19.1 cm (9½ x 7½"). Collection the artist

62 B. FIGURE 1 (from TEN NUMBERS). 1960. Charcoal on paper, 24.1 x 19.1 cm (9½ x 7½"). Collection the artist

62 C. FIGURE 2 (from TEN NUMBERS). 1960. Charcoal on paper, 24.1 x 19.1 cm (9½ x 7½"). Collection the artist

62 D. FIGURE 3 (from TEN NUMBERS). 1960. Charcoal on paper, 24.1 x 19.1 cm (9½ x 7½"). Collection the artist

62 E. FIGURE 4 (from TEN NUMBERS). 1960. Charcoal on paper, 24.1 x 19.1 cm (9½ x 7½"). Collection the artist

62 F. FIGURE 5 (from TEN NUMBERS). 1960. Charcoal on paper, 24.1 x 19.1 cm (9½ x 7½"). Collection the artist

62 G. FIGURE 6 (from TEN NUMBERS). 1960. Charcoal on paper, 24.1 x 19.1 cm (9½ x 7½"). Collection the artist

62 H. FIGURE 7 (from TEN NUMBERS). 1960. Charcoal on paper, 24.1 x 19.1 cm (9½ x 7½"). Collection the artist

62 I. FIGURE 8 (from TEN NUMBERS). 1960. Charcoal on paper, 24.1 x 19.1 cm (9½ x 7½"). Collection the artist

62 J. FIGURE 9 (from TEN NUMBERS). 1960. Charcoal on paper, 24.1 x 19.1 cm (9½ x 7½"). Collection the artist

63. DEVICE CIRCLE. 1960. Pencil on paper, 38.1 x 36.9 cm (15 x 14½"). Collection Mr. Ronald S. Lauder

64. JUBILEE. 1960. Graphite wash on paper, 79.7 x 63.7 cm (31⅜ x 25¹/₁₆"). The Museum of Modern Art, New York. Extended loan from the Lester and Joan Avnet Collection

65. OUT THE WINDOW. 1960. Charcoal and pastel on paper, 87.7 x 72.4 cm (34½ x 28½"). Collection Dr. and Mrs. Bernard Brodsky

66. PAINTING WITH TWO BALLS. 1960. Charcoal, pastel and pencil on paper, 49.6 x 38.7 cm (19½ x 15¼"). Joseph H. Hirshhorn Collection

67. THERMOMETER. 1960. Charcoal and pastel on paper, 56.5 x 41.9 cm (22¼ x 16½"). Collection the artist

68. 0 THROUGH 9. 1960. Charcoal on paper, 73.7 x 58.4 cm (29 x 23"). Collection the artist

69. TARGET. 1960. Lithograph (¹⁵/₃₀), 57.2 x 44.5 cm (22½ x 17½"). Published by Universal Limited Art Editions. Collection the artist

70. FLAG I. 1960. Lithograph (¹⁷/₂₃), 55.9 x 76.2 cm (22 x 30"). Published by Universal Limited Art Editions. Collection the artist

71. COAT HANGER I. 1960. Lithograph (²¹/₃₅), 91.4 x 67.9 cm (36 x 26¾"). Published by Universal Limited Art Editions. Collection the artist

72. 0 THROUGH 9. 1960. Lithograph (¹⁹/₃₅), 76.2 x 55.9 cm (30 x 22"). Published by Universal Limited Art Editions. Collection the artist

73. 0 THROUGH 9. 1961. Oil on canvas, 137.5 x 105.1 cm (54⅛ x 41⅜"). Hirshhorn Museum and Sculpture Garden, Smithsonian Institution, Washington, D.C.

74. 0 THROUGH 9. 1961. Oil on canvas, 137.2 x 114.3 cm (54 x 45"). Collection Carter Burden, New York

75. 0 THROUGH 9. 1961. Oil on canvas, 137.2 x 114.3 cm (54 x 45"). Collection Mr. and Mrs. S. I. Newhouse, Jr.

76. 0 THROUGH 9. 1961. Oil on canvas, 137.2 x 114.3 cm (54 x 45"). Collection Mr. and Mrs. Frank M. Titelman, Boca Raton, Fla.

77. MAP. 1961. Oil on canvas, 198.1 x 312.7 cm (78 x 123⅛"). The Museum of Modern Art, New York. Gift of Mr. and Mrs. Robert C. Scull, 1963

78. BY THE SEA. 1961. Encaustic and collage on canvas, 182.9 x 138.5 cm (72 x 54½"). Private collection, New York

79. LIAR. 1961. Encaustic, pencil, and sculp-metal on paper, 53.9 x 43.2 cm (21¼ x 17"). Collection Mr. and Mrs. Victor W. Ganz

80. IN MEMORY OF MY FEELINGS—FRANK O'HARA. 1961. Oil on canvas with objects, 101.6 x 152.4 cm (40 x 60"). Collection Dr. and Mrs. Eugene A. Eisner, Scarsdale, N.Y.

81. NO. 1961. Encaustic, collage, and sculp-metal on canvas with objects, 172.7 x 101.6 cm (68 x 40"). Collection the artist

82. GOOD TIME CHARLEY. 1961. Encaustic on canvas with objects, 96.5 x 61 cm (38 x 24"). Collection the artist

83. THE CRITIC SEES. 1961. Sculp-metal over plaster with glass, 8.2 x 15.8 x 5.4 cm (3¼ x 6¼ x 2⅛"). Private collection, New York

84. DEVICE. 1961–62. Oil on canvas with objects, 182.9 x 122.5 cm (72 x 48¼"). Dallas Museum of Fine Arts. Acquired in honor of Mrs. Eugene McDermott. Dallas Art Museum League, Mr. and Mrs. George V. Charlton, Mr. and Mrs. James B. Francis, Dr. and Mrs. Ralph Greenlee, Jr., Mr. and Mrs. James H. W. Jacks, Mr. and Mrs. Irvin L. Levy, Mrs. John W. O'Boyle, Dr. Joanne Stroud

85. 4 THE NEWS. 1962. Encaustic and collage on canvas with objects, 165.1 x 127.6 cm (65 x 50¼"). Private collection, New York

86. FOOL'S HOUSE. 1962. Oil on canvas with objects, 182.9 x 91.4 cm (72 x 36"). Collection Mr. Jean Christophe Castelli

87. ZONE. 1962. Oil, encaustic, and collage on canvas with objects, 153 x 91.5 cm (60 x 36"). Kunsthaus Zürich

88. PASSAGE. 1962. Encaustic and collage on canvas with objects, 137.2 x 101.6 cm (54 x 40"). Museum Ludwig, Cologne

89. OUT THE WINDOW NUMBER 2. 1962. Oil on canvas with objects, 182.9 x 121.9 cm (72 x 48"). Collection the artist

90. DIVER. 1962. Oil on canvas with objects, 228.6 x 431.8 cm (90 x 170"). The Albert A. List Family Collection

91. SLOW FIELD. 1962. Oil on canvas with objects, 182.9 x 91.4 cm (72 x 36"). Moderna Museet, Stockholm

92. FOLLY BEACH. 1962. Charcoal and pastel on paper, 90.2 x 73.7 cm (35½ x 29"). Anonymous collection

93. DISAPPEARANCE II. 1962. Ink on plastic, 45.7 x 45.7 cm (18 x 18"). Collection The Honorable and Mrs. Gilbert Hahn, Jr.

94. STUDY FOR SKIN I. 1962. Charcoal on paper, 55.9 x 86.4 cm (22 x 34"). Collection the artist

95. STUDY FOR SKIN II. 1962. Charcoal on paper, 55.9 x 86.4 cm (22 x 34"). Collection the artist

96. STUDY FOR SKIN III. 1962. Charcoal on paper, 55.9 x 86.4 cm (22 x 34"). Collection the artist

97. STUDY FOR SKIN IV. 1962. Charcoal on paper, 55.9 x 86.4 cm (22 x 34"). Collection the artist

98. PAINTING WITH TWO BALLS I. 1962. Lithograph (¹⁹/₃₉), 67.3 x 52.1 cm (26½ x 20½"). Published by Universal Limited Art Editions. Collection the artist

99. FALSE START I. 1962. Lithograph (¹²/₃₈), 75.6 x 56.5 cm (29¾ x 22¼"). Published by Universal Limited Art Editions. Collection the artist

100. FALSE START II. 1962. Lithograph (artist's proof), 78.7 x 57.2 cm (31 x 22½"). Published by Universal Limited Art Editions. Collection the artist

101. DEVICE. 1962. Lithograph (⁴/₆), 80 x 57.8 cm (31½ x 22¾"). Published by Universal Limited Art Editions. Collection the artist

102. 0–9. 1960–63. Ten lithographs from the portfolio 0–9 (B/C, 1/1, H.C.), each 52.1 x 40 cm (20½ x 15¾"). Published by Universal Limited Art Editions. Collection Mr. and Mrs. Leo Castelli

103. LAND'S END. 1963. Oil on canvas with objects, 170.2 x 121.9 cm (67 x 48"). San Francisco Museum of Modern Art. Gift of Mr. and Mrs. Harry W. Anderson

104. PERISCOPE (HART CRANE). 1963. Oil on canvas, 170.2 x 121.9 cm (67 x 48"). Collection the artist

105. MAP. 1963. Encaustic and collage on canvas, 152.4 x 236.2 cm (60 x 93"). Private collection

106. DIVER. 1963. Charcoal and pastel on paper, 219.7 x 180.3 cm (86½ x 71"). Collection Mr. and Mrs. Victor W. Ganz

107. UNTITLED. 1963. Charcoal, collage, and paint on paper, 108 x 76.2 cm (42½ x 30"). Collection Mr. and Mrs. Victor W. Ganz

108. HATTERAS. 1963. Lithograph ($^{16}/_{30}$), 104.7 x 75 cm (41¼ x 29½"). Published by Universal Limited Art Editions. Collection the artist

109. FIELD PAINTING. 1963–64. Oil on canvas with objects, 182.9 x 93.3 cm (72 x 36¾"). Collection the artist

110. ARRIVE/DEPART. 1963–64. Oil on canvas, 172.7 x 130.8 cm (68 x 51½"). Private collection, Munich

111. WATCHMAN. 1964. Oil on canvas with objects, 215.9 x 153 cm (85 x 60¼"). Collection Mr. Hiroshi Teshigahara, Tokyo

112. SOUVENIR. 1964. Encaustic on canvas with objects, 73 x 53.3 cm (28¾ x 21"). Collection the artist

113. SOUVENIR 2. 1964. Oil and collage on canvas with objects, 73 x 53.3 cm (28¾ x 21"). Collection Mr. and Mrs. Victor W. Ganz

114. ACCORDING TO WHAT. 1964. Oil on canvas with objects, 223.5 x 487.7 cm (88 x 192"). Collection Edwin Janss, Thousand Oaks, California

115. STUDIO. 1964. Oil on canvas with objects, 224.8 x 369.6 cm (88½ x 145½"). Whitney Museum of American Art. Gift of the Friends (and purchase)

116. ALE CANS. 1964. Lithograph ($^{3}/_{31}$), 57.2 x 44.5 cm (22½ x 17½"). Published by Universal Limited Art Editions. Collection the artist

117. UNTITLED. 1964–65. Oil on canvas with objects, 182.9 x 426.7 cm (72 x 168"). Stedelijk Museum, Amsterdam

118. SKIN WITH O'HARA POEM. 1963–65. Lithograph (artist's proof; ⅛), 55.9 x 86.4 cm (22 x 34"). Published by Universal Limited Art Editions. Collection the artist

119. HIGH SCHOOL DAYS. 1964. Sculp-metal over plaster with mirror, 10.8 x 30.5 x 11.5 cm (4¼ x 12 x 4½"). Collection the artist

120. SUBWAY. 1965. Sculp-metal over plaster and wood, 19.4 x 25.1 x 7.6 cm (7⅝ x 9⅞ x 3"). Collection the artist

121. FLAGS. 1965. Oil on canvas, 182.9 x 121.9 cm (72 x 48"). Collection the artist

122. EDDINGSVILLE. 1965. Oil on canvas with objects, 172.7 x 311.2 cm (68 x 122½"). Museum Ludwig, Cologne

123. PINION. 1963–66. Lithograph ($^{15}/_{36}$), 101.6 x 71.1 cm (40 x 28"). Published by Universal Limited Art Editions. Collection the artist

124. TWO MAPS I. 1965–66. Lithograph ($^{12}/_{30}$), 83.8 x 67.3 cm (33 x 26½"). Published by Universal Limited Art Editions. Collection the artist

125. PASSAGE II. 1966. Oil on canvas with objects, 151.8 x 158.8 cm (59¾ x 62½"). Harry N. Abrams Family Collection, New York

126. STUDIO 2. 1966. Oil on canvas, 177.8 x 317.5 cm (70 x 125"). Collection Mr. and Mrs. Victor W. Ganz

127. WATCHMAN. 1966. Graphite wash, metallic powder, pencil, and pastel on paper, 97.1 x 67.3 cm (38¼ x 26½"). Collection Mr. and Mrs. Victor W. Ganz

128. HARLEM LIGHT. 1967. Oil and collage on canvas, 198.1 x 436.9 cm (78 x 172"). Private collection

129. WATCHMAN. 1967. Lithograph ($^{3}/_{40}$), 91.4 x 61 cm (36 x 24"). Published by Universal Limited Art Editions. Collection the artist

130. TARGETS. 1967–68. Lithograph ($^{3}/_{42}$), 86.4 x 64.8 cm (34 x 25½"). Published by Universal Limited Art Editions. Collection the artist

131. 1ST ETCHINGS. 1967–68. Six etchings from the portfolio 1ST ETCHINGS ($^{8}/_{26}$), each 63.5 x 50.8 cm (25 x 20"). Published by Universal Limited

Art Editions. Whitney Museum of American Art. Gift of Mr. and Mrs. Stanley L. Helfgott

132. SCREEN PIECE. 1967. Oil on canvas, 182.9 x 127 cm (72 x 50"). Private collection

133. SCREEN PIECE 2. 1968. Oil on canvas, 182.9 x 127 cm (72 x 50"). Collection Mr. and Mrs. Victor W. Ganz

134. WALL PIECE. 1968. Oil and collage on canvas, 182.9 x 280 cm (72 x 110¼"). Collection the artist

135. EVIAN. 1968. Graphite, gouache, and pastel on paper, 76.2 x 53.9 cm (30 x 21¼"). Private collection

136 A. FIGURE 0. 1969. Lithograph ($^{1}/_{40}$), 96.5 x 78.7 cm (38 x 31"). Published by Gemini G.E.L. Collection the artist

136 B. FIGURE 1. 1969. Lithograph ($^{1}/_{40}$), 96.5 x 78.7 cm (38 x 31"). Published by Gemini G.E.L. Collection the artist

136 C. FIGURE 2. 1969. Lithograph ($^{1}/_{40}$), 96.5 x 78.7 cm (38 x 31"). Published by Gemini G.E.L. Collection the artist

136 D. FIGURE 3. 1969. Lithograph ($^{1}/_{40}$), 96.5 x 78.7 cm (38 x 31"). Published by Gemini G.E.L. Collection the artist

136 E. FIGURE 4. 1969. Lithograph ($^{1}/_{40}$), 96.5 x 78.7 cm (38 x 31"). Published by Gemini G.E.L. Collection the artist

136 F. FIGURE 5. 1969. Lithograph ($^{1}/_{40}$), 96.5 x 78.7 cm (38 x 31"). Published by Gemini G.E.L. Collection the artist

136 G. FIGURE 6. 1969. Lithograph ($^{1}/_{40}$), 96.5 x 78.7 cm (38 x 31"). Published by Gemini G.E.L. Collection the artist

136 H. FIGURE 7. 1969. Lithograph ($^{1}/_{40}$), 96.5 x 78.7 cm (38 x 31"). Published by Gemini G.E.L. Collection the artist

136 I. FIGURE 8. 1969. Lithograph ($^{1}/_{40}$), 96.5 x 78.7 cm (38 x 31"). Published by Gemini G.E.L. Collection the artist

136 J. FIGURE 9. 1969. Lithograph ($^{1}/_{40}$), 96.5 x 78.7 cm (38 x 31"). Published by Gemini G.E.L. Collection the artist

137. WALL PIECE. 1969. Pencil, graphite, pastel, watercolor, and collage on paper, 69.9 x 101.6 cm (27½ x 40"). Collection the artist

138. WALL PIECE. 1969. Ink on plastic, 68.6 x 94 cm (27 x 37"). Collection Mr. and Mrs. Victor W. Ganz

139. ZONE. 1969. Graphite, chalk, and gouache on paper, 83.2 x 44 cm (32¾ x 17⁵/₁₆"). Collection the artist

140. HIGH SCHOOL DAYS. 1969. Lead relief with mirror ($^{2}/_{60}$), 58.4 x 43.2 cm (23 x 17"). Edition of 60. Published by Gemini G.E.L. Collection the artist

141. BREAD. 1969. Lead relief with paper and paint ($^{28}/_{60}$), 58.4 x 43.2 cm (23 x 17"). Published by Gemini G.E.L. Whitney Museum of American Art. Gift of Howard and Jean Lipman Foundation, Inc.

142. THE CRITIC SMILES. 1969. Lead relief with gold and tin ($^{28}/_{60}$), 58.4 x 43.2 cm (23 x 17"). Published by Gemini G.E.L. Whitney Museum of American Art. Gift of Howard and Jean Lipman Foundation, Inc.

143. ENGLISH LIGHT BULB. 1968–70. Sculp-metal, wire, and polyvinyl chloride; dimensions variable—length of base 12.4 cm (4⅞"). Collection Mark Lancaster

144. VOICE 2. 1971. Oil and collage on canvas, three panels, each 182.9 x 127 cm (72 x 50"). Kunstmuseum Basel

145. DECOY. 1971. Oil on canvas with object, 182.9 x 127 cm (72 x 50"). Collection Mr. and Mrs. Victor W. Ganz

146. DECOY II. 1971–73. Lithograph ($^{3}/_{31}$), 104.1 x 73.7 cm (41 x 29"). Published by Universal Limited Art Editions. Collection the artist

147. UNTITLED. 1972. Oil, encaustic, and collage on canvas with objects, 182.9 x 487.7 cm (72 x 192"). Museum Ludwig, Cologne

148. TWO FLAGS. 1973. Oil and encaustic on canvas, 145.9 x 176.7 cm (57⁷/₁₆ x 69⁹/₁₆"). Collection Jacques Koerfer, Switzerland

149. UNTITLED. 1973. Oil and pencil on paper, 104.7 x 75 cm (41¼ x 29½"). Private collection

150. SKIN I. 1973. Charcoal on paper, 64.8 x 102.2 cm (25½ x 40¼"). Collection the artist

151. SKIN II. 1973. Charcoal on paper, 64.8 x 102.2 cm (25½ x 40¼"). Collection the artist

152. SCENT. 1973–74. Oil and encaustic on canvas, 182.9 x 320.6 cm (72 x 126¼"). Collection Ludwig, Aachen

153. TARGET. 1974. Encaustic and collage on canvas, 155.5 x 135.5 cm (61¼ x 53¼"). The Seibu Museum of Art, Tokyo

154 A. FACE. 1974. Lithograph (²/₄₉), 78.1 x 57.8 cm (30¾ x 22¾"). Published by Gemini G.E.L. Collection the artist

154 B. HANDFOOTSOCKFLOOR. 1974. Lithograph (²/₄₈), 78.1 x 57.8 cm (30¾ x 22¾"). Published by Gemini G.E.L. Collection the artist

154 C. BUTTOCKS. 1974. Lithograph (²/₄₉), 78.1 x 57.8 cm (30¾ x 22¾"). Published by Gemini G.E.L. Collection the artist

154 D. TORSO. 1974. Lithograph (²/₅₀), 78.1 x 57.8 cm (30¾ x 22¾"). Published by Gemini G.E.L. Collection the artist

154 E. FEET. 1974. Lithograph (²/₄₇), 78.1 x 57.8 cm (30¾ x 22¾"). Published by Gemini G.E.L. Collection the artist

154 F. LEG. 1974. Lithograph (²/₅₀), 78.1 x 57.8 cm (30¾ x 22¾"). Published by Gemini G.E.L. Collection the artist

154 G. KNEE. 1974. Lithograph (²/₄₇), 78.1 x 57.8 cm (30¾ x 22¾"). Published by Gemini G.E.L. Collection the artist

155. CORPSE AND MIRROR. 1974. Oil, encaustic, and collage on canvas, 127 x 173 cm (50 x 68⅛"). Collection Mr. and Mrs. Victor W. Ganz

156. CORPSE AND MIRROR II. 1974–75. Oil on canvas with painted frame, 146.4 x 191.1 cm (57⅜ x 75¼"). Collection the artist

157. CORPSE. 1974–75. Ink, Paintstik, and pastel on paper, 108 x 72.4 cm (42½ x 28½"). Collection the artist

158. UNTITLED. 1974–75. Watercolor and Paintstik on paper, 62.9 x 51.4 cm (24¾ x 20¼"). Collection Janie C. Lee

159. THE DUTCH WIVES. 1975. Encaustic and collage on canvas, 131.4 x 180.3 cm (51¾ x 71"). Collection the artist

160. THE BARBER'S TREE. 1975. Encaustic and collage on canvas, 87 x 137.8 cm (34¼ x 54¼"). Collection Ludwig, Aachen

161. WEEPING WOMEN. 1975. Encaustic and collage on canvas, 127 x 259.7 cm (50 x 102¼"). Private collection, New York

162. FOUR PANELS FROM UNTITLED (1972). 1975. Lithograph (A/D, B/D, C/D, D/D; each ¹/₂₀), four panels, each 104.1 x 81.3 cm (41 x 32"). Published by Gemini G.E.L. Collection the artist

163. SCENT. 1975–76. Lithograph, linocut, and woodcut (³/₄₂), 79.3 x 119.4 cm (31¼ x 47"). Published by Universal Limited Art Editions. Collection the artist

164. CORPSE AND MIRROR. 1976. Silkscreen (⁸/₆₅), 109.2 x 135.2 cm (43 x 53¼"). Published by Simca Print Artists, Inc. Collection the artist

165. END PAPER. 1976. Oil on canvas, 152.4 x 176.6 cm (60 x 69½"). Private collection